If They Can Argue Well, They Can Write Well

Using classroom debate to teach students to write persuasively, think critically, and research and evaluate Internet sources

By
Dr. Bill McBride

Incentive Publications
Nashville, Tennessee

**"Americans need not only personal
morality, but gifted tongues as well."**

—*Gary Fine*

Illustrated by Kathleen Bullock
Cover by Geoffrey Brittingham
Edited by Jill Norris
Copyedited by Cary Grayson

ISBN 978-0-86530-692-9

3   4   5   6   7   8   9   10   11

Printed by Sheridan Books, Inc., Chelsea, Michigan • August 2011
www.incentivepublications.com

Table of Contents

Part 3: Learning to Think Critically

Part 4: Learning to Write Persuasively

Teacher's Final Grading and Conference Rubric

Additional Resources

An Opening Argument from the Author:

The Rationale to Support the Contention
If They Can Argue Well, They Can Write Well

If you've ever raised or taught a teenager, you've probably heard or taken part in a conversation like the one below:

"Sarah, have you done your homework?"
"Mom, I have to go to the mall!"
"Why?"
"Because I HAVE to."
"What does going to the mall have to do with your homework?"
"Because all the other girls said they'd meet me there."
"Yes, but what about your homework?"
"Mom, the sale started today. Do you want me to look like a Neanderthal?"
"Where did you learn the word 'Neanderthal'?"
"Mom, I'm not totally stuuuupid. I learned it in band."
"Band?"
"Yeah, Mr. Douglas said I played like a Neanderthal."
"And what did you say?
"I said, 'Thanks.' You taught me to be polite. Okay, I'll see ya later."
"Homework?"
"I promise to do anything you ask when I get back. Bye!"

Let's face it. One thing teens can, and often do, is argue. They argue with their siblings, with their peers, with their teachers, and especially with their parents. Have you ever listened to a teen give a myriad of reasons to do, or not do something? You were probably thinking one of two thoughts:

One — "That last reason made absolutely no sense."

Two — "Why doesn't she put this kind of energy into her schoolwork?"

The intent of this book is to tackle these two issues—to encourage students to think logically and put more time and energy into their schoolwork. More specifically, it involves teaching them to think critically about taking a stance and then, structuring their arguments into powerful, persuasive essays.

Arguing is natural to teens and begins early in childhood. William Corsaro (2003) notes in his comparative research of young children

that conflict contributes to the social organization of peer groups, the development and strengthening of friendship bonds, the reaffirmation of cultural values, and the individual development and display of self.
(p. 162)

These same characteristics of conflict appear in adolescents. Any parent can tell you that sometimes teens seem to *argue just for the sake of arguing.* Adolescence is a time when teens define themselves by seeking independence from their parents and guardians. They are often more influenced by the interests, beliefs, and values of their peers than by their parents. Teens also argue to defend who they think they are. If a teen says he's a vegetarian, he may use argumentation to define, explain, and even persuade others about his lifestyle choice.

Teens argue as a form of problem solving in order to understand how life works in their cultural and social environment. What teen hasn't argued the question of "fairness"? For example, a teen may say, "You said if I did my homework that I could go to the mall. All of my friends are going. Now you say you need me to watch after Jamie. How is that fair?"

Most prominently perhaps, adolescents use argumentation to determine their status among their peers. In the movie "8 Mile," Eminem enters rap "debates" to win a place of respect among African-American rappers. Teens may "diss" or "disrespect" each other by using put-downs. The "winner" gains a place of power among peers because few teens, or any of us for that matter, want to be humiliated in front of others.

Argument and Academics

When we overhear teens argue in school, whether it is part of a classroom discussion or a hallway clash, it is often no more than one assertion followed by a lot of *ad hominem* name-calling—not unlike certain talk shows. Most of our students don't even know how to argue well. Deanne Kuhn (2005) at Columbia University states in her book *Education for Thinking*,

> Argument is ubiquitous in people's lives, and the case is compelling that students need to learn to argue well, that doing so is critical education for life. Yet relatively little attention has been paid to the path from arguing to arguing well that we would like to see students navigate. (p. 117)

Our students' inability to reason and argue well is captured by Gerald Graff (2003) in his book *Clueless in Academe: How Schooling Obscures the Life of the Mind*. The author points out that in many social situations people aren't even sure if they are having a conversation, a debate, or an argument. As an example, he presents this famous Monty Python comedy sketch entitled "The Argument Clinic" from the British TV show of the '70s (Paramount Pictures, 1970).

> A man appears at a clinic and announces that he is looking for an argument. He is directed to Office 12, whereupon opening the door he is met with a stream of insults and invective from the functionary behind the desk:
>
> "You snotty-nosed piece of parrot-droppings. . . . Your type makes me puke. You vacuous, toffee-nosed, malodorous pervert."
>
> "What's this? I came here for an argument."
>
> "Oh, I'm sorry. This is Abuse. You want 12A next door."
>
> Going to the office next door, the client asks the man at the desk if this is the Argument Department.
>
> "I told you once . . ."
>
> "'No, you didn't."
>
> "Yes, I did."
>
> "Did not."
>
> "Did . . ."
>
> Finally, the client objects that "this isn't argument, just mere contradiction."
>
> "No, it isn't."
>
> "Yes, it is. An argument is a connected series of statements leading to a definite proposition."
>
> "No, it's not . . ."
>
> "Argument is an intellectual process, not an automatic gainsaying of anything the other person says."
>
> "Not necessarily."

Kuhn (2005) partly attributes the lack of students' ability to reason and argue well as a reflection of our society. Politicians, marketing specialists, pollsters, and the media inundate our young with *what* people think rather than *why*. Reasoned argument, including counterarguments and rebuttals, are "not highly valued in much of American culture" (p. 117). Reasoned debate doesn't fit the Evening News time slot as well as a sound byte. Kuhn points out that many teachers may be uncomfortable with discussion because they are unable to control its direction or goal.

> *Teachers' concern to ensure students "learn something" is fed, perhaps, by their uncertainty as to what discussion itself has to teach them. One possibility to consider is that teachers would be more comfortable with a wider range of discussion topics— some "academic" and some not—to the extent that they had a clearer sense of the goals to which these discussions should aspire. (p. 116)*

Teachers may also be fearful to initiate discussions of high interest topics due to the pressure they feel to cover state and district standards in order to raise test scores. The desire to "cover the material" creates a school culture in which "breadth" outweighs "depth." Giving students time to research topics and develop thoughtful arguments does not fit well into today's curricula. Teachers who sense they have limited instructional time and abundant content resort to promoting superficial memorization of concepts or procedures rather than deep student discussion and critical analysis. Thus, *chalk and talk* preempts *research and reflect*.

A further outcome from rapidly covering large amounts of material is the loss of student engagement. In the study *The Silent Epidemic*, funded by the Bill and Melinda Gates Foundation, 47 percent of students claimed they dropped out because they were bored, while 69 percent said they were "not motivated or inspired to work hard." Nearly 90 percent had passing grades when they quit. (Bridgeland *et al*, 2006) Mike Schmoker, in his book *Results Now*, cites a study of 1,500 classroom observations in which 85 percent of the classes had fewer than one-half of the students paying attention. (2006, Learner 24/7, 2005) Students today see little connection between the memorization of subject matter to pass a test and the technological world in which they live—a world that entertains with continuous choices, feedback, relevance, and challenges at the touch of a finger.

Keeping argument out of the classroom is just another indication to students that school is artificial and doesn't represent the real world. As Gerald Graff (2003) notes,

> *Schools should be tapping far more than they do into students' youthful argument cultures, which are not as far removed as they look from public forms of argument . . . instead of taking advantage of the bridges between youthful argument worlds and those of public discourse, schools generally make it hard for students to recognize their argumentative practices in those of academia. At worst, students get the impression that to do well in school or college they have to check whatever argumentative inclinations they have at the classroom door. (pp. 155–156)*

Channeling Confrontation in the Classroom

The question then arises: Is there a way to rethink our curriculum in such a way that argumentation, critical thinking, and standards can be met in an engaging format? Three years ago I read in the *Journal of Adult and Adolescent Literacy* an interesting study by Mark Felton and Suzanne Herko entitled "From Dialogue to Two-sided Argument: Scaffolding Adolescents' Persuasive Writing". (2004) In their study, Felton and Herko created a sequenced method to use a teen's natural desire to argue in the classroom as a lead-in to writing, or as they state, "to build on students' oral debate skills to strengthen their written assignments" (Felton, Herko, p. 672).

The idea of using debate as a lead-in to writing makes sense on a number of levels. First, debate is engaging because it is competitive. Gary Fine (2001) writes in his book *Gifted Tongues: High School Debate and Adolescent Culture* that "the model of debate as a game (or sport) challenges and motivates adolescents for whom the spice of competition enlivens the presentation of arguments" (p. 42).

For teenagers, knowing that they will be standing in front of their peers to compete against each other is a powerful motivator. New research in genetic gender differences in brain development indicates that boys' brains are drawn to competition. (Sax, 2005; Gurian, 2005) Since males make up the vast majority of our school failures and dropouts, finding ways to engage them makes sense.

Similar to Fine's conclusions, Kuhn (2005) found in a study that using debate in two middle school classrooms heightened engagement for many reasons.

> Students were engaged and attuned to a shared activity in a way that was not typical during other class periods. One factor certainly was the competitive one—one team was going to win and the other lose. But beyond

that, I think, was the satisfaction most of these students derived from being able to express an opinion and be listened to, in a context that was officially sanctioned—they were not 'talking out of turn,' as was usually the case whenever they expressed themselves during class time. Most of the school day for these students was about being quiet, following instructions, and complying with demands. Rarely in their school lives, and most likely in their lives outside of school, did they have the experience of expressing a significant idea and being listened to and taken seriously. (p. 119)

Giving students an opportunity to express a significant idea implies that they must also have time to prepare, to research, to analyze data, and to present their findings. In other words, when preparing for a debate, students must exhibit many of the same skills required to prepare a good persuasive essay.

> Debate involves not only the acquisition of knowledge, but a set of verbal and research skills that all persons, not only debaters, use: techniques of persuasion and reasoning. To be competent, one must acquire information-processing skills: the ability to gather, organize, and present information. To induce another to ratify one's claims demands facility with words and line of discourse, and to counter alternate arguments. Learning how to talk—to argue, to counter, and to persuade—is such a critical skill that an explicit focus on how this skill is acquired seems valuable but, surprisingly, has been largely ignored. (Fine, 2001, p. 6)

Mike Schmoker agrees.

> Given a good text, an arresting issue, students like to argue, in small groups or as a class. We're daft if we don't see that argument teaches them to think and is about the best

inducement we have for getting them to read purposefully and write with passion and energy—in class, where they can feel the energy of one another's ideas and worldviews. (2006, pp. 71–72)

But will it work? Does implementing structured argumentation actually build critical thinking and increase student engagement and achievement? Perhaps one of the best examples of success is Deborah Meier's work at Central Park East Secondary School (CPESS) in East Harlem. Meier made intellectual issues and debates a core part of both faculty and student work, placing them on a level with sports and adolescent socialization. In her book, *The Power of Their Ideas* (2002) she describes how this challenging academic perspective worked with her 450 seventh-through-twelfth graders. The result was that 90 percent of CPESS students went directly into college and stayed there while the New York City average graduation rate was only 50 percent.

Mike Schmoker (2007) in a recent article in *Educational Leadership* describes the successes of Tempe Preparatory Academy in Phoenix—an open-enrollment charter school whose population consists mostly of middle and lower-middle class families. When Arizona administered its first AIMS standards test six years ago, Arizona students scored terribly low; but 100 percent of the Tempe students passed. What is different about this curriculum? In two words: "argumentative literacy" (Graff, 2003). As Schmoker notes,

Students analyze and argue, agree or disagree with the ideas they encounter, and evaluate the ethics of various characters' actions. And—significantly—students' work incorporates mastery of Arizona's standards for language arts:

displaying logic and clarity, making inferences, doing character analysis, supporting one's arguments, synthesizing, evaluating, and discerning an author's bias or perspective. (2007, p. 64)

Based on evidence that reasoned debate might be one answer to developing critical thinking, engaging adolescents, and raising levels of achievement, I began workshopping the concept with middle and high school faculties across the country three years ago. During these workshops, I asked teachers of language arts, debate, and social studies, as well as assorted specialists from the real world of the classroom, to help me modify the original concept—to give it the additional scaffolding that students need in order to move from an oral debate to a well-crafted persuasive essay. This book is the result of that input and my own teaching experience. The lessons are designed to be immediately useful to the teacher. The process of taking students from a debate to a well-written essay is provided almost completely in copy master form. Based on brain research, the lessons are designed so that students are physically and emotionally engaged throughout the process, not just staring blankly at a sheet of paper or a computer screen for long periods of time. The four parts of the book are described on the following pages along with relevant research that helps confirm the instructional steps as best practices.

An Overview of this Book for the Teacher:

Research Findings that Support Using Debate to Teach Persuasive Writing

Part 1:
Learning to Argue

"Students need to become sold on the idea of school and its purposes. They need to become convinced that we are not wasting their time" (Kuhn, 2005).

Part 1: Learning to Argue is scaffolded into eleven steps. Both the methodology for teaching the steps and the reproducible student activity pages that scaffold instruction are provided.

Step 1: Learning the Language of Debate
Step 2: Grading a Student's Persuasive Paper
Step 3: Separating Fact and Opinion
Step 4: Analyzing an Opinion or Claim
Step 5: Identifying Opposing Arguments and Rebuttals
Step 6: Reading the Research
Step 7: Choosing Your Contentions
Step 8: Fighting Their Counterarguments
Step 9: Understanding the Steps of Debate
Step 10: Taking Notes on a Debate
Step 11: Choosing Your Topic to Debate

Debate by nature involves controversial issues; consequently, a **Letter to Parents about this Lesson** is included, as well as the list of debate topics from which students will choose. The letter reminds parents that democracy itself is dependent on a critically thinking populace that is willing to debate, listen, and compromise. It is highly recommended that this letter be given to both your students' parents and your principal so that they are aware of what you are teaching.

Scaffolded Lessons

In **Step 1: Learning the Language of Debate** students are introduced to relevant academic vocabulary they will need to understand in order to complete the activities. This step includes simplified definitions of the

terms, a *Word Wall* activity to teach them, and two review and reteaching activity sheets.

Then, in the spirit of "backward design," students begin with what they will be asked to produce in the end—a persuasive essay. In **Step 2**, they are asked to grade holistically on a scale of 1 to 5 a student essay on the topic of "Off-Campus Lunch." On the first reading, most students give the essay good to excellent marks, usually a 4 or a 5. At this point, however, many have little idea of what constitutes a well-written persuasive essay.

Good persuasive essays should make claims that include warrants, such as an explanation of the casual link between the claim and the support. Crammond (1998) carried out a study in which two

10

sixth grade classes wrote persuasive essays on the same topic as seven professional writers to see what differences emerged. She found that many students either did not recognize they needed to make strong claims with supporting evidence or they did not know how to articulate these claims.

As Crammond suggests, students need to know the elements of a good persuasive essay and identify those elements in model essays. In a discussion of the teaching of writing in schools, Michael Schmoker (2006) notes that "most [students] are never given multiple, carefully-sequenced opportunities to practice these individual elements, to receive feedback, and to study good examples that make these elements clear" (p. 95).

Consequently, **Steps 3, 4,** and **5** provide well-structured graphic organizers that show students how to analyze the essay they've just graded for

- facts versus opinions,
- the elements of a well-supported opinion, and finally,
- counterarguments and rebuttals.

When students are asked to reevaluate the same essay, scores take a dramatic drop. As they move through the steps of part one, students are beginning to deduce what constitutes a well-supported argument.

To keep students engaged, they will next participate in a debate about the death penalty. To help students see that an oral argument requires the same kind of support that the sample essay lacked, the class reads two well-supported models on the death penalty in **Step 6.** Once they've decided where they stand

on the issue, they'll use graphic organizers in **Steps 7** and **8** to note their arguments and opposing views. In **Step 9** students are introduced to a simplified debate structure. (In workshops with teachers, it was decided to keep the debate structure uncomplicated so that students wouldn't get overly focused on the procedure, instead of forming their arguments.) At this point the teacher selects four class members to debate the death penalty while the rest of the class uses the **Step 10** graphic organizer to take notes on their performance and choose a winner.

Now that students have seen a model of debate that they will later perform, they are ready to choose their own topics to research in **Step 11**. Topics that work well in the classroom require a few constraints:

- First, they need be "deep" enough so that students can find significant support, as well as contrary opinions. For example, the topic of "Wearing Hats in School" may be of high interest to students; however, little research would be available.
- Second, students need to pick topics that are appropriate for the diversity of the classroom.

Finding a balance between topics that students might actually be interested in researching and "intellectual ideas appropriate for school" is difficult. Graff (2003) reminds us, however, that the process is more important than the product. Relying on topics that are deemed "intellectual" at the cost of losing student engagement sabotages the entire method. As Graff (2003, p. 213) notes,

We associate the life of the mind too exclusively with subjects and texts that we precategorize as weighty in

themselves. We assume that it is possible to wax intellectually about Plato, Shakespeare, the French revolution, and nuclear fission; but not about cars, clothing fashions, dating, sports, TV, or Bible belt religion. However, no necessary relationship has ever been established between any text or subject and the educational depth and weight of the discussion it can provoke. Real intellectuals turn any subject into grist for their mill through the thoughtful questions they bring to it, whereas dullards will find a way to drain the richest subject of interest.

Based on these constraints and the recommendations of debate teachers from around the country, a set of 25 topics is provided from which students may select one they'd like to debate. Your students are now ready to research their topics.

Part 2:
Learning to Research

"A capacity for autonomous learning and a thirst for unending education are more important than accurate recall or simplistic application of the particular knowledge taught" (Wiggins, 1993).

Part 2: Learning to Research is scaffolded into the following ten steps.

    Step 1:   Learning the Language of Research
    Step 2:   Using On-line Reference Works
    Step 3:   Researching with Search Engines
    Step 4:   Practicing Boolean Searching
    Step 5:   Evaluating a Web Site
    Step 6:   Learning About Surveys
    Step 7:   Conducting a Survey
    Step 8:   Analyzing Your Data
    Step 9:   Researching Your Topic
    Step 10: Researching Their Counterarguments

Scaffolded Lessons

Again, in **Step 1** students always begin by learning relevant academic terms, in this case about the research process. One can't debate well without doing research. Unfortunately, research by many of today's students is often a three-step process: Google It, Cut and Paste It, Turn It In. Consequently, **Steps 2, 3,** and **4** teach students how to use online reference tools, such as encyclopedias, dictionaries, and almanacs, how to use Internet search engines, and how to do Boolean searching. Each step includes online activities to practice these new skills. Because adolescents are renowned for simply copying information off the Internet without evaluating either the information or its source, **Step 5** provides information and activities on how to evaluate web sites, as well as two different evaluation matrices for their use.

As students research, much of the data that they encounter is in the form of surveys; hence, it is important that they understand this mode of research. In **Steps 6** and **7,** students learn how surveys are constructed and then, to promote engagement, carry out their own class survey on afterschool activities. To understand the most common statistics presented in research, a basic math lesson is provided in **Step 8** on the mean, median, mode, and range, and how to figure percentages. Your class then applies their math skills to analyze their classroom survey data.

Students are NOW ready to start researching their topics for debate. **Steps 9** and **10** provide the graphic organizers for students to note both their contentions, or claims, and possible counterarguments. Noting counterarguments is a recognized weakness that occurs when students build their own arguments. (Kuhn, 1991, 1997; Crammond, 1998; Felton & Herko,

2004) Deanna Kuhn, in particular, notes the value of having students discover opposing opinions.

> *Paradoxically, to know that a theory is correct entails the ability to envision and address claims that it may not be. It matters little how many alternative theories are successfully rebutted and rejected, if one's own theory remains unexamined. . . . That it is easier to find fault with the other person's view than with one's own is perhaps not surprising. Yet both of these forms of bias are significant, in that they reflect limitations in people's abilities to evaluate their own beliefs and, hence, to know that they are justified in holding them. (p. 171)*

Your students are now gathering data, but they still need to learn how to think critically about the information they find.

Part 3:
Learning to Think Critically

"Free access to information is essential, but no more important than the intellectual capacity to make sense of that information: to think, discern, and make distinctions that inform our conversations, our decisions, how we vote" (Schmoker, 2006).

Part 3: Learning to Think Critically is scaffolded into the following fourteen steps.

Step 1: Learning the Language of Logic
Step 2: Understanding Reasoning
Step 3: Learning About Logical Fallacies
Step 4: Identifying Logical Fallacies
Step 5: Understanding Persuasive Techniques
Step 6: Identifying Persuasive Techniques
Step 7: Analyzing Bias and Loaded Language
Step 8: Building a Strong Case
Step 9: Planning Your Debate Offense
Step 10: Building a Strong Rebuttal
Step 11: Planning Your Debate Defense
Step 12: Following the Steps of Debate
Step 13: Taking Notes on a Debate
Step 14: Evaluating Your Debate

Scaffolded Lessons

As in every part of the book, students begin in **Step 1** by learning important academic terms about critical thinking. One of the values of debate is that it lets students see these terms come alive in a safe, structured activity. In *The Debater's Guide,* (2003, p. 3-4) John Ericson, James Murphy, and Raymond Zeuschner list the intellectual attributes of any good debater:

- The ability to collect and organize ideas.
- The ability to subordinate ideas.
- The ability to evaluate evidence.
- The ability to see logical connections.
- The ability to think and speak in outline terms and identify the relationships between items.
- The ability to speak convincingly and
- The ability to adapt.

These intellectual abilities are similar to the critical thinking skills that Wiggins (1993), Meier (2002), and others call the *Habits of Mind.* The habits of mind are sixteen mental dispositions that promote a productive learning environment.

People who possess and use these dispositions habitually tend to be successful at problem solving and attaining goals. As Michael Schmoker states: "Every day of their school lives, students should be reading texts critically, then weighing evidence for or against people, ideas, and policies, and forming opinions. These activities foster a set of essential, intellectual 'habits of mind' . . ." (2006, p. 55).

The list below identifies these sixteen habits of mind as described by Arthur Costa and Bena Kallick in *Assessing & Reporting on Habits of Mind* (2000,

pp. 52–53). I've put a star in the second column if research shows the process of debate process fosters a particular habit of mind.

Habit of Mind	The Process of Debate
Exhibit persistence	*
Manage impulsivity	*
Listen with understanding and empathy	*
Think flexibly	*
Think about your own thinking	*
Strive for accuracy	*
Question and pose problems	*
Think and communicate with clarity and precision	*
Apply past knowledge to new situations	*
Take responsible risks	*
Create, imagine, and innovate	*
Think interdependently	*
Remain open to continuous learning	*
Respond with wonderment and awe	probably
Find humor	probably
Gather data through all the senses	probably

To teach students these habits of mind, **Step 2** provides instruction and models of inductive and deductive reasoning. **Steps 3** and **4** provide instruction in logical fallacies and practice in identifying them. In the "NAEP Facts" report on Persuasive Writing, students are recommended to "choose an approach they will use. They may, for instance, use emotional or logical appeals . . ." (p. 3, NAEP 2000). Consequently, **Steps 5** and **6** provide instruction in persuasive, or propaganda, techniques as well as practice in identifying them in class and in the real world of the media. **Step 7** shows students how to identify bias and the negative and positive connotations found in loaded language. Students are also asked to look back at their own research on their topic of debate to identify fallacies and bias to plan how they can use persuasive methods to make their summaries more powerful.

Thus far students have successfully researched their topics, have taken notes on their research, have evaluated the sources of their information, and have learned about potential weaknesses and strengths in their thinking. They are now ready to build their argument. Again, appropriate step-by-step scaffolding is provided. First, in **Step 7** students learn how to choose the strongest evidence. They then outline their own evidence in **Step 8**. Students are also reminded that they must read any research that argues against their topic so that they can rebut counterarguments. **Step 9** shows the differences between weak and strong rebuttals. Students then outline possible counterarguments and their rebuttals in **Step 10**.

Your students are now ready to hold their debates. **Step 12** reminds them of the simplified structure they will follow. (Debates normally take between 15 and 20 minutes.) To keep the entire class engaged, **Step 13** provides a note-taking sheet for those not debating so that they can keep track of arguments in order to vote on a winner.

Wiggins (1993) notes that

> It is not the student's errors that matter, but the student's responses to error; it is not mastery of a simplistic task that impresses, but the student's risk taking with the inherently complex; it is not thoroughness in a novice's work that reveals understanding, but full awareness of the dilemmas, compromises, and uncertainties lurking under the arguments he or she is willing to tentatively stand on. (p. 67)

Consequently, to aid students in such self-assessment, **Step 14** requires those who debated to look back at their performance and recognize any concessions, qualifications, and reservations they need to make in their arguments. It is suggested that teachers let the four students debate one more time in front of the class before beginning to write their persuasive essays.

Part 4:
Learning to Write Persuasively

————————

"Unless we produce some problem, trouble, or instability, we have no excuse for writing at all" (Graff, 2003).

————————

Part 4: Learning to Write Persuasively is scaffolded into the following eight steps.

Step 1:   Learning the Language of Writing
Step 2:   Organizing Your Essay
Step 3:   Outlining Your Essay
Step 4:   Varying Your Sentences
Step 5:   Grabbing Your Reader from the Start
Step 6:   Paraphrasing, Not Plagiarizing
Step 7:   Revising Your Paper
Step 8:   Citing Your Internet Sources

————————

Our students tend to write much in the same way they argue—not well. As Felton and Herko (2004) note, "A typical, single conversational turn in argumentative dialogue contains little more than a position statement supported by one or two claims—precisely what we find in poorly written essays" (p. 673).

Poorly written persuasive essays proliferate in our public and private schools. Our state and national test scores reflect the difficulty our students have in writing, which reflects how well we teach it. Though persuasive writing in particular is one of the most tested modes of writing on high stakes tests, our students continue to do poorly. In the 2002 National Assessment of Educational Progress (NAEP) tests, 72 percent of fourth graders, 69 percent of 8th graders, and 77 percent of 12th graders scored Below Proficient on the writing segment (NAEP, 2002). These scores showed small increases from the 1998 tests; however, the fact that so many of our students write so poorly is disheartening. (Note: As of this writing, the 2006 NAEP scores had not been published.)

As a former English and social studies teacher and language arts textbook editor, I am personally aware of the difficulty in getting students to write well. I am convinced that one of the main reasons writing instruction fails is because students are not emotionally invested in the process. Brain-based research clearly shows the need for students to be engaged in their learning. Our long-term memories are, in fact, stored in the emotional center of our brain (Jensen, 1998; Sousa, 2001). Yet writing classes often consist of long lectures or readings about writing followed by long periods of silence as students write. The National Writing Project and the Writing Workshop approach have made headway by adding conversations about writing to the process, but still too often students are not engaged in their writing, or lose their engagement somewhere along the way, especially when the topics are chosen for them. All the writing classes in the world won't improve our students' writing if they are not emotionally invested in the work.

One reason students don't write well is because they are not given the opportunity to make the connection between conversation and composition. As Graff (2003) notes,

> The idea that discourse is inherently 'dialogical,' that we internalize external conversation in virtually everything we say, has been developed in various ways by influential thinkers such a Bakhtin, Rorty, Derrida, McIntyre, and Vygotsky. The idea is implicit in Kenneth Burke's celebrated depiction of intellectual history as an endless parlor conversation into which as individuals we drop in and out. (p. 158)

With the improvements in the students' writing in their own study, Felton and Herko (2004) concluded that "By drawing on students' experience in oral argumentation, we can help them better understand the structure of their written arguments. By having them test their written arguments in oral debate, we make the critical audience come alive" (p. 682).

The previous three sections of the book have led your students to this point where they have gathered information, evaluated their sources, taken notes on both sides of their issue, and thought critically about these notes. Most importantly, however, they have had a chance to rehearse their ideas in oral argument. This final part of the book, **Learning to Write Persuasively,** will walk them through the steps of turning these concepts and skills into a well-written paper.

Scaffolded Lessons

As always, in **Step 1** students learn the academic vocabulary used in writing persuasively. In **Step 2** students choose one of two different structures to organize their essays. Based on their choice, **Step 3** guides them through the process of transferring their notes into an outline. The best essays are written by people who have also acquired their own individual style and voice. To help students become more creative writers, models on varying their sentence structures and practice on beginning an essay with an attention-getting opener are provided in **Steps 4** and **5**.

As most teachers will concede, one of the greatest problems with students writing expository pieces is **plagiarism**. **Step 6** shows students the differences between *plagiarism* and *paraphrasing* and provides practice with this skill. Now that students have begun writing, **Step 7** provides them with a rubric with which they can self-assess. The rubric may also be used in peer review for formative assessment. Finally, **Step 8** instructs students how to cite sources both within their papers and at the end. Once papers are finished, a final **Teacher Grading and Conference Rubric** is provided for summative assessment of the writing.

"Sarah, you need to do your homework!"
  "Why?"

"Because you need to do your homework."
  "Mom, that's just circular reasoning."

"If you don't get your homework done now, you won't get it done."
  "Now Mom, you're only avoiding the issue by offering an either/or alternative."

"I'm not avoiding any issue. If you stop doing your homework your life will crumble."
  "Seriously, Mom, you don't think I'm falling for that slippery slope."

"Don't you want to keep up with all your classmates who do their homework?"
  "Bandwagon, Mom. Hello!"

"I bet Maria has already done her homework."
  "Oh, and now it's product comparison."

"Listen here, you smart aleck. I've had enough. Little Ms. Genius can sit down right now and get to work."
  *"Well, if you're going to resort to **ad hominem** name calling!"*

–Bill McBride

Acknowledgments
Great teaching is an ongoing process of trial and error with an ever-changing student population. Our best ideas are often built on the best practices of others. I owe great thanks to the work of researchers such as Deanna Kuhn and Mark Felton as well as educators such as Gerald Graff, Gary Fine, and Mike Schmoker. I also owe great thanks to many teachers who suggested practical classroom methods to get students to argue well, to research well, to think critically, and to write persuasively. My only fear is that this methodology might work too well. Just think about it, what if teens really CAN argue back intelligently? As they say on their screens: OMG!

PART 1
LEARNING TO ARGUE

FOR THE TEACHER

FOR THE STUDENT

LEARNING TO ARGUE

In Learning to Argue, students will evaluate a student's sample paper, read research on the death penalty, learn to take notes on research, debate this issue in front of each other, and finally, pick a topic they will research and later write about. (You may want to copy the Teacher Directions pages to use as a guide.)

– Teacher Directions –

Before you begin this lesson, read the important note to teachers and the letter to parents that follow the directions.

Step 1: Begin by teaching the academic vocabulary students will need to know to understand the debate process. Step 1 provides the directions for doing a Word Wall activity with these words. Reproduce the activity sheet (page 26) **Learning the Language of Debate** so that students can record their definitions. Use the two practice activity sheets for reviewing these definitions (pages 27 and 28).

Step 2: In order to implement a "backward design," reproduce and distribute the activity sheet (page 29) **Grading a Student's Persuasive Paper**. Have students read and score the essay about off-campus lunch.

Step 3: Now have students analyze the student essay. Have them fill out the activity sheet (page 30) **Separating Fact and Opinion**. (Students will find few facts as they do their analysis.)

Step 4: Tell students that opinions are fine if they are well supported. Pass out the activity sheet (page 31) **Analyzing an Opinion or Claim** and have students look for facts, research, surveys, quotes by experts, and real-world examples. (Again, they will find few.)

Step 5: Explain to students that a good argument acknowledges counterarguments and offers rebuttals to them. Reproduce and distribute the activity sheet (page 32) **Identifying Opposing Arguments or Rebuttals** for students to fill out. (Again, they will find few.) Now ask students to reevaluate the student paper. (Most will give it a lower score.)

Step 6: Tell students they will now read a well-supported argument on the death penalty. First, however, they are going to literally see where they stand on this issue. Ask students to think about whether they believe in the death penalty or not and to write down two reasons they believe the way they do. Now ask students who **Strongly Agree** with it to move to one corner. Ask students who **Somewhat Agree** to move to a different corner. Ask students who **Strongly Disagree** to move to a third corner. Finally, ask students who **Somewhat Disagree** to move to the final corner. Call on students from each corner to give some reasons why they believe the way they do.

In order to complete **Reading the Research**, reproduce and distribute the two articles (pages 33 and 34). Give the article "Death Is What They Deserve" to those that agree killing a killer is correct. Give the article "The Death Penalty IS Cruel and Unusual" to those that disagree.

Step 7: Have students read their articles independently. Distribute copies of the activity sheet **Choosing Your Contentions** (page 36). Pair up like-minded students to complete this worksheet, deciding their four strongest points, or contentions, and what evidence they have to support those contentions.

Step 8: Tell students that they need to prepare for what the other team will say to tear down their arguments. Students now read the essay that opposes their view on the death penalty. Then, distribute the activity sheet **Fighting Their Counterarguments** (page 37). Tell students to considering what the opposing team will say against their ideas and how to answer those arguments as they complete the activity sheet.

Step 9: You are now ready to hold a "20-Minute Debate." Distribute copies of the activity sheet **Understanding the Steps of a Debate** (page 39). Allow all students to rehearse their responses for a few minutes. Then choose two opposing pairs to debate and walk them through the following sequence. (Choose students who will probably be successful so that students see a good model of debating.) Here is the best procedure to follow:

1) The first **affirmative** speaker states and briefly explains two reasons, or contentions, to support the proposition.

2) IMPORTANT: The second **affirmative** speaker writes these two points on the board.

3) The first **negative** speaker FIRST counters the two reasons given by the affirmative side, and then gives two reasons for opposing the proposition. Allow the two teams to confer. *(You may also want the nonspeaking member of each team to copy down the other team's counterarguments. Writing the arguments in another color is visually helpful.)*

4) IMPORTANT: The second **negative** speaker writes their two points on the board.

5) The second **affirmative** speaker counters the new opposing positions of the negative side, and then gives two final reasons for supporting the proposition.

6) The first speaker of the **affirmative** side writes their new contentions on the board.

7) The second **negative** speaker counters the final two points of the affirmative side, and then gives the final two contentions for opposing the proposition.

8) The first **affirmative** speaker refutes the negative claims and gives a final emotional summary.

9) The first **negative** speaker refutes the affirmative claims and gives a final emotional summary.

Step 10: BEFORE the debate begins, distribute copies of the activity sheet **Taking Notes on a Debate** (page 40). Tell the students that they are required to fill out this sheet during the debate. Now begin the debate. Feel free to stop the teams at any time to help them follow the sequence. Allow opposing teams to discuss how to refute the other team's contentions.

Step 11: Once the debate is finished, have students vote for the team they think won. Then tell students they are going to choose a topic they will debate in front of their classmates. Distribute copies of the activity sheet **Choosing a Debate Topic** (page 41) and follow its instructions. Use the **Teacher's Tally Sheet** (pages 42 and 43) to pair up students.

Setting up teams: You will need two pairs to debate each topic. Because each student chooses five topics, you should be able to build the teams easily. Try to let them be on the *agree* or *disagree* side they chose. This creates more emotional engagement. Place any extra students on a team of three and let the teammates later decide which two will actually debate. Pair students who can work well together.

IMPORTANT NOTE TO TEACHERS

You are about to embark on one of the most dynamic units you may ever implement with your students—instructing them how to think thoughtfully about important ideas and express those ideas coherently in the form of debate. Such instruction may seem frightening to some parents. Parents are often fearful that teachers preach a particular stance to their children. This is NOT the intent of this unit. It is designed to show students how to evaluate and express two sides of an issue.

Recently, however, court decisions have begun to limit the freedom of speech of teachers in the classroom. On Jan. 24, 2007, a three-judge panel in the Seventh U.S. Circuit Court of Appeals stated, "The Constitution does not entitle teachers to present personal views to captive audiences against the instruction of elected officials [i.e., the School Board]" (Egelko, 2007).

To safeguard your role as a teacher, please do the following before teaching this unit:

1. Notify your principal that you will be teaching a unit on debate that includes a few controversial issues. Tell him that students choose their topics and parents approve them.

2. As you move through the unit, always make sure multiple points of view are given equal time for expression, unless those comments are rude or inappropriate.

3. Never let a student feel ostracized for accepting a particular position or pressured to accept a particular point of view as their personal belief.

4. Never disclose your personal feelings on an issue in school. At one point students will vote on who wins their debates. The program is set up so that students will vote by filling out a secret ballot, thus safeguarding their confidentiality.

5. Have students take home to their parents a copy of the letter on page 23. The letter explains the value of this unit. Give your principal a copy of the letter. Ask parents to sign the letter and return it to you.

6. If a parent objects to their child taking part, offer the child an alternative activity during a particular debate, or if necessary, another way to complete the research, critical thinking, and writing of the persuasive paper.

Dear Parent or Guardian,

The United States of America is founded on the principle of democracy. True democracy requires that educated people debate hard issues and come to decisions that benefit citizens. As Thomas Jefferson, the writer of our Declaration of Independence, said, "I know of no safer depository of the ultimate powers of the society but the people themselves; and if we think them not enlightened enough to exercise their control with a wholesome discretion, the remedy is not to take it from them, but to inform their discretion by education."

Your child is about to begin a unit in which he or she will learn the following:
- How to think critically about local, national, and world issues
- How to find evidence to support a particular view he or she has chosen
- How to evaluate evidence as to its honesty and validity
- How to stand up and present a viewpoint in a debate
- How to argue against views he or she disagrees with
- How to write that viewpoint in a well-constructed persuasive essay.

American citizens must possess these skills if democracy is to survive. In the beginning of this unit, your child will choose a topic to debate in front of his or her classmates. The list of topics is attached to this letter. Please review this list. If you have any concerns or do not wish your child to be exposed to BOTH sides of any particular issue, please let the teacher know, and an alternative topic or assignment will be given.

Once you've reviewed the list, please sign this letter and return it to school.

Sincerely,

Parent or Guardian's Signature: _____

Date: _____

Topics for Debates

DIRECTIONS: Your child will pick a topic from this list to debate in front of the class. Students will each choose five topics they would like to study. The teacher will select from these five the one topic which your child will debate, but all students will study BOTH sides of any issue. Please put a check by any topics on this list that you don't want your child to debate in class. Contact your child's teacher if you have any other concerns.

1. _____ Resolved: Students learn and behave better when wearing uniforms.

2. _____ Resolved: Single-sex schools help students learn better than co-ed schools.

3. _____ Resolved: College players should be paid for postseason tournaments.

4. _____ Resolved: Corn-based ethanol should replace gasoline in ten years.

5. _____ Resolved: America's invasion of Iraq has done more harm to the world than good.

6. _____ Resolved: No illegal immigrants should be allowed into the United States.

7. _____ Resolved: Students should be allowed to use cell phones in school.

8. _____ Resolved: The age to get a driver's license should be 18.

9. _____ Resolved: Marijuana should be legalized.

10. _____ Resolved: People who are gay should be allowed to marry.

11. _____ Resolved: Racial profiling of people who look like terrorists is necessary in today's world.

12. _____ Resolved: Rap songs with violent lyrics should be censored.

13. _____ Resolved: Stricter gun control will decrease gun-related crimes.

14. _____ Resolved: All abortion should be illegal.

15. _____ Resolved: English should be made the official language of the United States.

16. _____ Resolved: Student athletes should be allowed to take fewer courses.

17. _____ Resolved: LeBron James is a greater basketball player than Michael Jordan.

18. _____ Resolved: Teachers should be paid on their ability, not years of service.

19. _____ Resolved: Historically, the UNC Tar Heels have the best college basketball program.

20. _____ Resolved: Athletes proven to have taken steroids should be banned from the record books and the Hall of Fame.

21. _____ Resolved: Doctors should be allowed to help the terminally ill die.

22. _____ Resolved: Violent video games do not promote violent behavior.

23. _____ Resolved: Fast-food chains should be banned from school cafeterias.

24. _____ Resolved: Genetically engineered food should be banned.

25. _____ Resolved: Historically, the NBA Los Angeles Lakers are the greatest professional basketball team.

LEARNING THE LANGUAGE OF DEBATE
Using a Word Wall to Learn Academic Terms

1. Begin teaching the academic terms for debate on a Monday. Write each of these terms on a large sheet of construction paper and tape them up on the wall. Reproduce the record sheet *Learning the Language of Debate* on page 26 for individual students.

2. At the beginning of Monday's class, distribute the *Learning the Language of Debate* record sheet. Don't define the words in the order they appear on the page. Instead, choose the simplest word that you think most of your students will know. Point to the word on your Word Wall and ask if anyone can define that word. Get as many definitions as you can from your students. Then decide on one simple definition that everyone understands. As you write this definition on the board, have students copy it onto their form. Continue until all the words are defined. If no one knows the definition of a word, speak aloud sentences with clear context clues until the students can infer the definition. For example, you might say, *My sister always has to give me her **opinion** about my clothes. She tells me exactly how she feels about what I wear. What is an **opinion**?*

3. At the beginning of Tuesday's class, tell students to get out a blank sheet of paper and number it from 1 to 15. Beginning with the simplest word, call out the definitions created on Monday. Ask students to "Write down the word that means . . . ." Students are NOT allowed to look at their definitions. Ask them how they did at the end and then move on with your lesson.

4. On Wednesday repeat the same procedure as on Tuesday—call out the definitions, have students find the correct word on the wall, and record it on their numbered papers. Make sure to call out the definitions in a different order. Distribute copies of **Practice 1** (page 27) and have students complete the page.

5. On Thursday repeat the same procedure as on Wednesday—call out the definitions, have students find the correct word on the wall, and write it down. Call the definitions in a different order. Distribute copies of the crossword puzzle (page 28) and have students complete the page.

6. On Friday repeat the same procedure one more time, calling the definitions in yet another order. Explain to students that this is their *test*. Most likely EVERY ONE of your students will get 100 percent and know how to spell the words correctly.

Simplified Definitions of Terms:

1. debate – to argue both sides of a topic
2. fact – something proven to be true
3. opinion – a feeling or belief
4. quote – to write exactly what someone said
5. resolve – make a firm decision to do something
6. proposition – a subject to be debated
7. evidence – facts and examples that prove something
8. persuade – to try to convince someone
9. contention – a strong statement to support one side of an argument
10. affirmative side – side that supports the proposition
11. negative side – side that opposes the proposition
12. oppose – to be against something
13. rebuttal – a response to a counterargument
14. concede – to admit that someone else is right
15. counterargument – an opposing argument or response

Name: _____

Learning the Language of Debate

TERM	DEFINITION
1. debate	
2. fact	
3. opinion	
4. quote	
5. resolve	
6. proposition	
7. evidence	
8. persuade	
9. contention	
10. affirmative side	
11. negative side	
12. oppose	
13. rebuttal	
14. concede	
15. counterargument	

Learning the Language of Debate

DIRECTIONS: Read each sentence below. The underlined words give a definition or example for one of the vocabulary words. Write that word in the blank provided.

1. _____ Mary had <u>a feeling or belief</u> that her math teacher was excellent.

2. _____ Our class decided <u>to argue the two sides of the issue</u> of the death penalty.

3. _____ Maria <u>tried to convince</u> her mother to buy the dress.

4. _____ My father <u>made a firm decision about what he was going to do</u>.

5. _____ Tom, my brother, always <u>takes a side against me</u> when playing chess.

6. _____ The lawyer in the murder case had to present <u>facts and examples to prove his point</u>.

7. _____ Sheila wrote down <u>exactly what the teacher said</u> to study for the test.

8. _____ For every reason I gave my mom, she gave <u>an opposing answer</u>.

9. _____ Our class chose teenage drinking as <u>a subject to be discussed and analyzed</u>.

10. _____ In our classroom debate, Jeremy and Leticia were <u>on the side that agreed with the proposition</u>.

11. _____ In contrast, Stacey and Mark were <u>against the proposition</u>.

12. _____ It <u>can be proven to be true</u> that candy is sweeter than lettuce.

13. _____ Every time I offered a counterargument to my dad's reasons to clean my room, he would <u>give a response that destroyed my argument</u>.

14. _____ David <u>gave a strong statement or assertion to support his side of the argument</u>.

15. _____ I have <u>to admit that part of your argument is correct</u>.

Debate Crossword

Across

5. to admit that someone else is right
8. an opposing argument or response
12. side that opposes the proposition
13. to write exactly what someone said
14. a strong statement to support one side of an agrument
15. to argue both sides of a topic

Down

1. a response to a counterpoint
2. a feeling or belief
3. something proven to be true
4. a subject to be debated
6. facts and examples that prove something
7. to try to convince someone
9. to be against something
10. make a firm decision to do something
11. side that supports the proposition

Grading a Persuasive Essay

DIRECTIONS: Read this persuasive essay written by a student. Give it a quick score by circling one of the numbers below. A score of 1 is "terrible," 3 is "average," and 5 is "excellent."

1   2   3   4   5

Let's Get Out and Eat Out!
A Persuasive Paper on Off-Campus Lunch

Imagine sitting in the same loud location eating the same kind of foul food for four years of your life. That's what it's like at our high school. We are not allowed to go off campus for lunch. There are a lot of reasons we should have off-campus privileges at lunchtime. We would get better quality food. We would get a break from our teachers, and we would have more time. Also, if we didn't have to eat junk for food, our students would be happier and do better work.

The quality of the food in the cafeteria is bad. No one really likes eating the food there. Most feel it tastes like newspaper. There is just no flavor to anything, unless you consider a lot of salt as flavor. Mr. Jackson, an English teacher, said the food there is not good for us. If we could go to nearby restaurants we could get real food. For example, McDonald's and Taco Bell are right across the street with better tasting food. You can smell the glorious grilling of beef in our halls.

Another reason we should be allowed to go off campus is to get a break from our teachers. When someone is having a bad day, it's good to get away for a while. Even a break of 20 minutes can improve your mood. This break isn't just good for the students. I bet the teachers would like a break from us too, especially since they wouldn't have to do lunch duty where they just yell at kids.

The last reason we need an off-campus lunch is to have more time to eat. Some principals will say it would take too long for us to eat off campus. They think if students go to restaurants no one will ever eat in the cafeteria again and people will lose their jobs. So, most of our lunch time is spent standing in a huge line. By the time we get our food, we have to shove it down in order to get to the next class. If we had off-campus lunch, less people would be in line at any one place.

Why can't students eat hot, moist burgers or spicy tacos instead of putrid peas? Students would get a break from their teachers. We'd have time to relax and digest our food. Come on, everyone. Tell the administration. I say, "Let's get out and eat out!"

Name: _____

Separating Fact and Opinion

When writers want to persuade you to believe something, they normally include both facts and opinions to convince you. It is important to understand the difference.

- A **fact** is something that can be proved to be true. For example, it is a fact that there are 12 inches in a foot. It is a fact that Cuba is an island.

- An **opinion** is a personal belief or feeling. For example, it is an opinion that college basketball is the most exciting sport to watch. It is an opinion that pizza is always good.

DIRECTIONS: Reread the essay about "Off-Campus Lunch." As you read, list the **facts** stated by the author in the left-hand column. List the **opinions** in the right-hand column.

Facts	Opinions

You probably found more opinions than facts.
How might this affect your support of a writer's beliefs?

Analyzing an Opinion or Claim

How do you know whether to believe someone's opinion? To support an opinion well, writers should give evidence to convince you that their opinion is correct. This evidence usually includes proven facts or figures, scientific research, and real-world examples as evidence.

DIRECTIONS: Now reread the essay on "Off-Campus Lunch" again. Yes, AGAIN! This time, use the chart below to analyze how well the writer has supported his opinion.

1. What opinion is the writer stating?
2. What facts does the writer give to support the opinion?
3. What scientific research, statistics, surveys or quotes from experts are given?
4. What real-world examples are given that support this opinion?

Based on your findings, does the writer's opinion seem to be well-supported?

If They Can Argue Well, They Can Write Well
Copyright ©2008 by Incentive Publications, Inc., Nashville, TN _____

Name: _____

Identifying Opposing Arguments and Rebuttals

A well-constructed argument recognizes opposing opinions. The writer then has a choice to either state, in a rebuttal, that the opposing views are incorrect, or to agree, or concede, with the opposing views, even in a limited way.

DIRECTIONS: Reread the essay on "Off-Campus Lunch" one last time. Use the chart below to list any opposing views given by someone else. If the writer gave a rebuttal to the opposing view, list it also. **After you've finished, score the essay again at the bottom of this page.**

Writer's View:

Opposing Views or Counterarguments:

1. _____
2. _____
3. _____
4. _____
5. _____
6. _____
7. _____

Writer's Rebuttals to Counterarguments:

1. _____
2. _____
3. _____
4. _____
5. _____
6. _____
7. _____

My new score is _____ .

Did your score change? If so, how and why?

If They Can Argue Well, They Can Write Well
Copyright ©2008 by Incentive Publications, Inc., Nashville, TN

Reading the Research—Affirmative

DIRECTIONS: You are going to debate the death penalty before your fellow students. To prepare for this debate, you need to read some research. If you are **FOR** the death penalty, or having killers put to death, read the essay below.

Death Is What They Deserve
(In Support of the Death Penalty)

The death penalty has been used since the dawn of time as a means of punishing criminals. Some crimes, especially murder, are so horrible that the death penalty seems the only fair punishment. Many people may argue that capital punishment is not moral, but it was not moral of the criminal to commit the crime in the first place, therefore, swift punishment is appropriate. The death penalty shows that murder is not to be tolerated and will be punished in an appropriate manner.

The death penalty is also a way to deter potential murderers and criminals, or make them think twice before killing for fear of losing their own life. This is known as the "deterrence" factor. In 1973, Isaac Ehrlich was able to prove that for every inmate who was executed, seven lives were spared because others were stopped from committing murder. Other studies have been done which show the same results. Those who oppose this view try to find statistics to support the idea that capital punishment does not deter crime. They also suggest that states in the United States that do not use the death penalty have lower murder rates. Vicious murderers must be killed to prevent them from murdering again, either in their prison or out in society, if they were paroled. Opponents to this idea will argue that most murderers do not expect to get caught when committing a crime and that most crimes are committed in moments of anger. But most studies show that deterrence has a strong effect on criminals. The death penalty helps society to prevent any future crimes.

Many argue that the death penalty is based on discrimination against African Americans, but in fact, more white people than black people are executed. The Supreme Court rejected the use of statistical studies, which claim racism as the sole reason for abolishing the death penalty. Opponents try to prove that blacks are executed more than white criminals. There have been a few studies that attempt to prove that, but mostly they do not take into account other influential factors.

Another thing to be considered is the high cost factor of keeping criminals alive, as opposed to using the death penalty. Many criminals cannot afford the cost of attorneys, and the State must bear the burden of the cost for the criminal. It is not easy to calculate the final costs of a trial, judge, prosecutor (most often appointed by the State) and other court officials. A recent trial of Tavara Wright cost the state of Texas approximately $200,000 for two separate trials, with a third trial waiting. It is even more costly to keep criminals alive in prisons and on Death Row. It costs over $19,000 a year to keep a criminal in prison. Opponents attempt to prove just the opposite, that it costs more to execute a criminal than to have him or her in prison for life. It is easy to use facts and figures to an advantage. Money taken out of the pocket of taxpayers either way is money that could be used in better ways for the good of society.

According to a 1994 Gallup poll, 74 percent of Americans support the death penalty. It is a just and fair way to deal with criminals. It helps to prevent future crimes and it is rooted in religious beliefs. It is the best way to deal with those who choose to murder and take innocent lives.

WORKS CITED

"The Death Penalty." Michigan State University Comm Tech Lab and Death Penalty Center. 23 Jan 2007.
   http://www.deathpenaltyinfo.msu.edu

"News From the U.S. Supreme Court." 23 Jan 2007. **http://www.deathpenaltyinfo.org/article.php?did=248&scid=38**

"The Death Penalty—arguments for and against capital punishment." 23 Jan 2007. **http://www.findarticles.com**

"Recent Background News on Death Penalty". News Batch. 25 Jan 2007. **http://www.newsbatch.com/deathnews.html**

Forsberg, Mary E. "Money for Nothing: The Financial Cost of New Jersey's Death Row." November 2005.
   25 Jan 2007. **http://www.njpp.org/rpt_moneyfornothing.html**

Name: _____

Reading the Research—Negative

DIRECTIONS: You are going to debate the death penalty before your fellow students. To prepare for this debate, you need to read some research. If you are **AGAINST** the death penalty, or against having killers put to death, read the essay below.

The Death Penalty IS Cruel and Unusual
(In Opposition to the Death Penalty)

Capital punishment, or the death penalty, is a barbaric and ancient practice. Very few civilized countries still practice putting someone to death for a crime. Only countries such as Iraq, Iran, and Korea still practice this horrible form of cruel and unusual punishment. America is one of the only countries in the western world that has not yet abolished the death penalty. Opponents feel that capital punishment is just another word for revenge, and fails to support the highest ideals of our culture. Letting executions continue is just another form of "payback." We need to behave in a civilized manner to continue to be a civilized society.

There is little, if any, proof that executions of criminals deter, or make them think twice about committing a crime. In fact the best conclusion is that the death penalty is no more effective than a sentence to life in prison. Studies that attempt to prove the opposite are not well documented and have not been given much credit. One fact that is clear is that states in the United States that don't use the death penalty have a lower murder rate than states that do use capital punishment. One survey shows that the South accounts for 80 percent of executions and yet has the highest murder rate in the United States. This proves the fact that criminals are not deterred by threat of the death penalty. And the United States has a higher murder rate than European countries, which don't use the death penalty. Proponents of the "deterrence" idea often use Isaac Ehrlich's outdated study of 1973, which showed that for "every inmate who was executed, seven lives were spared because others were 'deterred' from committing murder." This study is too old to be used as evidence in our modern days. Criminals do not expect to get caught, tried, and punished, and so they don't consider the differences between a possible execution and life in prison. Former Texas Attorney General Jim Mattox said, "It is my own experience that those executed in Texas were not deterred by the existence of the death penalty law." The death penalty is a step backward.

The death penalty also discriminates against those who cannot afford the best defense lawyers and do not have access to the best courts and trial procedures. Many lawyers are so inexperienced they are completely unprepared to defend the criminal, and that criminal is therefore more likely to be tried, convicted, and given a death sentence. This is especially true when it comes to the racial issue. Blacks are sentenced more frequently than whites. Proof of this is that since 1976, when the death penalty was reinstated in the United States, 202 black criminals have been executed for the murder of a white victim, but only 12 white defendants have been executed for the death of a black person. Opponents cite the decision of the Supreme Court not to use race as the single reason for overturning a death sentence, but race is part of other factors, such as poverty.

Finally, the recent use of DNA testing has helped prove that many criminals who were convicted and put on Death Row were, in fact, innocent. It is interesting to note, according to a 1987 study, that between 1900 and 1985 over 350 people were eventually found innocent of their crimes. If DNA testing had been used in cases tried in the 1970s and 1980s, some of the convicts probably would have been found innocent. Even more alarming is the fact that recently 23 criminals were found innocent of their crimes after they had been put to death, using scientific equipment and DNA test procedures. Opponents argue that while DNA may be used, it is not perfected yet, and other factors must be considered first in deciding the death penalty. They feel that the need to reform our court system is not a reason to abolish the death penalty. But it is very important that all criminals be given all available resources, including experienced defense attorneys, non-racist juries, and the very latest scientific evidence, including DNA testing.

There is no doubt that the death penalty, as it is currently being used in the United States, is a cruel and unusual punishment, often to innocent people. It is an ancient ritual that needs to be abolished.

WORKS CITED

"The Death Penalty." Michigan State University Comm Tech Lab and Death Penalty Center. 21 Jan 2007.
    http://www.deathpenaltyinfo.msu.edu
"The Death Penalty—arguments for and against capital punishment." 23 Jan 2007. **http://www.findarticles.com**
    "News From the U.S. Supreme Court." 23 Jan 2007. **http://www.deathpenaltyinfo.org/article.php?did=248&scid=38**
        "Recent Background News on Death Penalty." News Batch. 25 Jan 2007. **http://www.newsbatch.com/deathnews.html**
            "Death Penalty Focus." FACTS. 25 Jan 2007. **http://www.deathpenalty.org/index/php?pid=facts&menu=1**

Choosing Your Contentions
Page 1

DIRECTIONS: For your debate you will need strong supporting points, or contentions, to prove that your feelings on the death penalty are correct. Reread your essay on the death penalty. Use the page below to note your first two contentions and the evidence you found for each point. (It is a good idea to begin with your strongest point.)

Your 1st Contention or Claim:

Evidence (facts, research, statistics, surveys, real-world examples) to support this point:

_____

_____

_____

_____

_____

_____

_____

Your 2nd Contention or Claim:

Evidence (facts, research, statistics, surveys, real-world examples) to support this point:

_____

_____

_____

_____

_____

_____

_____

Choosing Your Contentions
Page 2

DIRECTIONS: Use the page below to note your third and fourth contentions and the evidence you can find to support your reasons.

Your 3rd Contention or Claim:

Evidence (facts, research, statistics, surveys, real-world examples) to support this point:

_____

_____

_____

_____

_____

_____

_____

Your 4th Contention or Claim:

Evidence (facts, research, statistics, surveys, real-world examples) to support this point:

_____

_____

_____

_____

_____

_____

_____

Fighting Their Counterarguments
Page 1

DIRECTIONS: Now you need to guess how your opponent in the debate will counter, or tear down your argument. Begin by reading the other essay that you disagree with. Once you see a counterargument, or something the other team will say against you, write it down in the **Counterargument** space. Then decide how to answer their point. Write this down in the **Rebuttal** space.

Your 1st Contention or Supporting Reason:

Their Opposing Views or Counterarguments:

-
-
-
-

Your Rebuttals to Counterarguments:

-
-
-
-

Your 2nd Contention or Supporting Reason:

Their Opposing Views or Counterarguments:

-
-
-
-

Your Rebuttals to Counterarguments:

-
-
-
-

Fighting Their Counterarguments
Page 2

DIRECTIONS: Use the page below to note your third and fourth contentions, possible counterarguments to your opinions, and how you will answer them.

Your 3rd Contention or Supporting Reason:

**Their Opposing Views
or Counterarguments:**

-
-
-
-

**Your Rebuttals
to Counterarguments:**

-
-
-
-

Your 4th Contention or Supporting Reason:

**Their Opposing Views
or Counterarguments:**

-
-
-
-

**Your Rebuttals
to Counterarguments:**

-
-
-
-

Understanding the Steps of Debate

DIRECTIONS: You're about to watch a class debate. This chart will show you the steps a debate follows. Follow the arrows below to see how a debate takes place.

Affirmative Side

Negative Side

1st Speaker
- States Proposition
- Argues Two Contentions

2nd Speaker
- Records Affirmative Contentions on Board

1st Speaker
- States Any Counterarguments
- Argues Two Contentions

2nd Speaker
- Records Negative Contentions on Board

2nd Speaker
- States Any Counterarguments
- Argues Two New Contentions

1st Speaker
- Records New Affirmative Contentions on Board

2nd Speaker
- States Any Counterarguments
- Argues Two New Contentions

1st Speaker
- Records New Negative Contentions on Board

1st Speaker
- States Any Counterarguments
- Offers Final Rebuttals of All Negative Claims
- Gives Final Persuasive Summary

1st Speaker
- Offers Final Rebuttals of All Affirmative Claims
- Gives Final Persuasive Summary

Name: _____

Taking Notes on a Debate

DIRECTIONS: Use this form to take notes on your classmates' debates.

Proposition of Debate: _____

_____

_____

Debaters: Affirmative Side _____ _____

Negative Side _____ _____

Your opinion before the debate: _____

_____

Affirmative Side Contentions and Evidence:	Negative Side Contentions and Evidence:
●	●
●	●
●	●
●	●

Your opinion after the debate: _____

_____

Check whom you think won the debate: Affirmative _____ Negative _____

Choosing Your Topic to Debate

DIRECTIONS: You're now ready to pick a topic you will debate in front of the class. Read the list of topics below. Decide on the top five topics you are most interested in. Write a 1 by your favorite, 2 by your next favorite, and so on. **Choose the topic and NOT how it is stated.** If you agree with the statement, put an "**A**" by your number. If you disagree with the statement, put a "**D**" by your number.

1. _____ Resolved: Students learn and behave better when wearing uniforms.

2. _____ Resolved: Single-sex schools help students learn better than co-ed.

3. _____ Resolved: College players should be paid for postseason tournaments.

4. _____ Resolved: Corn-based ethanol should replace gasoline in ten years.

5. _____ Resolved: America's invasion of Iraq has done more harm to the world than good.

6. _____ Resolved: No illegal immigrants should be allowed into the United States.

7. _____ Resolved: Students should be allowed to use cell phones in school.

8. _____ Resolved: The age to get a driver's license should be 18.

9. _____ Resolved: Marijuana should be legalized.

10. _____ Resolved: People who are gay should be allowed to marry.

11. _____ Resolved: Racial profiling of people who look like terrorists is necessary in today's world.

12. _____ Resolved: Rap songs with violent lyrics should be censored.

13. _____ Resolved: Stricter gun control will decrease gun-related crimes.

14. _____ Resolved: All abortion should be illegal.

15. _____ Resolved: English should be made the official language of the United States.

16. _____ Resolved: Student athletes should be allowed to take fewer courses.

17. _____ Resolved: LeBron James is a greater basketball player than Michael Jordan.

18. _____ Resolved: Teachers should be paid on their ability, not years of service.

19. _____ Resolved: Historically, the UNC Tar Heels have the best college basketball program.

20. _____ Resolved: Athletes proven to have taken steroids should be banned from the record books and the Hall of Fame.

21. _____ Resolved: Doctors should be allowed to help the terminally ill die.

22. _____ Resolved: Violent video games do not promote violent behavior.

23. _____ Resolved: Fast-food chains should be banned from school cafeterias.

24. _____ Resolved: Genetically engineered food should be banned.

25. _____ Resolved: Historically, the NBA Los Angeles Lakers are the greatest professional basketball team.

Choosing Your Topic to Debate

DIRECTIONS: Use this sheet to tally what choices your students made. Pair up students who picked similar topics and who will work together well. **Remember that you need four students per topic—two for the Affirmative and two for the Negative. Don't be afraid to switch a pair from the Affirmative to Negative side for the sake of a good argument!**

TOPIC   STUDENT TEAMS

1. _____ Resolved: Students learn and behave better when wearing uniforms.

2. _____ Resolved: Single-sex schools help students learn better than co-ed.

3. _____ Resolved: College players should be paid for postseason tournaments.

4. _____ Resolved: Corn-based ethanol should replace gasoline in the next ten years.

5. _____ Resolved: America's invasion of Iraq has done more harm to the world than good.

6. _____ Resolved: No illegal immigrants should be allowed into the United States.

7. _____ Resolved: Students should be allowed to use cell phones in school.

8. _____ Resolved: The age to get a driver's license should be 18.

9. _____ Resolved: Marijuana should be legalized.

10. _____ Resolved: People who are gay should be allowed to marry.

11. _____ Resolved: Racial profiling of people who look like terrorists is necessary in today's world.

12. _____ Resolved: Rap songs with violent lyrics should be censored.

Choosing Your Topic to Debate

	TOPIC	STUDENT TEAMS

13. _____ Resolved: Stricter gun control will decrease gun-related crimes. _____ _____ / _____ _____

14. _____ Resolved: All abortion should be illegal. _____ _____ / _____ _____

15. _____ Resolved: English should be made the official language of the United States. _____ _____ / _____ _____

16. _____ Resolved: Student athletes should be allowed to take fewer courses. _____ _____ / _____ _____

17. _____ Resolved: LeBron James is a greater basketball player than Michael Jordan. _____ _____ / _____ _____

18. _____ Resolved: Teachers should be paid on their years of service, not on how good they are. _____ _____ / _____ _____

19. _____ Resolved: Historically, the UNC Tar Heels have the best college basketball program. _____ _____ / _____ _____

20. _____ Resolved: Athletes proven to have taken steroids should be banned from the record books and the Hall of Fame. _____ _____ / _____ _____

21. _____ Resolved: Doctors should be allowed to help the terminally ill die. _____ _____ / _____ _____

22. _____ Resolved: Violent video games do not promote violent behavior. _____ _____ / _____ _____

23. _____ Resolved: Fast-food chains should be banned from school cafeterias. _____ _____ / _____ _____

24. _____ Resolved: Genetically engineered food should be banned. _____ _____ / _____ _____

25. _____ Resolved: Historically, the NBA Los Angeles Lakers are the greatest professional basketball team. _____ _____ / _____ _____

PART 2
LEARNING TO
RESEARCH

FOR THE TEACHER

FOR THE STUDENT

LEARNING TO RESEARCH

In Learning to Research, students will learn how to do Internet research, how to evaluate their sources, how to collect data on the research topic they chose in Part I, how to conduct surveys, and how to analyze data. They will then begin researching their topics, studying both sides of their issues.

Step 1: Begin by teaching the academic vocabulary students will need to know to understand the research process. To use a Word Wall and daily activities, see page 47 for notes. Individual students can record the definitions on **Learning the Language of Research** (page 48). Use the two practice sheets (pages 49 and 50) to review and reinforce these definitions.

Step 2: Tell students that they will begin to do research to build their argument so that they can WIN their debate. Remind them that they could go to the Library or Media Center and look up their subject in encyclopedias and other reference books. Since these books may have been printed over a year ago, however, it is possible that the information is not up to date. Tell them they can also find many of these same resources on-line. Two reproducible pages (pages 51 and 52) provide a list of major online reference books.

Step 3: Tell students that reference works like encyclopedias give lots of general information on a topic. They will also want to find current magazine and journal articles that have more up-to-date information. To find the most current information, they'll need to do a more intensive search of the Internet. Reproduce and distribute **Researching with Search Engines** (pages 53 and 54) to show students how to use Internet search engines.

Step 4: Students need additional practice with using searching engines. Reproduce and distribute **Practicing Boolean Searching** (page 55) to help them refine their Internet searches.

Step 5: Many students have no idea how to evaluate the information they find on the Internet. Guide students through the six-step evaluation process **Evaluating a Web Site** (pages 53–59) to model how to check the reliability and validity of their Internet sources.

Step 6: Tell students that they will probably find surveys that support or oppose their opinions. Use the information sheet **Learning**

About Surveys (pages 60 and 61) to teach students about sample groups, how to make a questionnaire, and how people generalize based on the data from surveys.

Step 7: To maintain student engagement, they will now conduct their own survey on afterschool activities. The **Survey Tally Sheets** (pages 62 and 63) are included to control the "choices" of activities students record.

Step 8: Tell students that once they've collected data, or information, they need to study it to understand what they've found out. If their information is in the form of written responses, then they should look for patterns, or similar responses that are repeated. If their information is numerical, they can use math to see patterns. Reproduce and distribute **Analyzing Your Data** (pages 64–66). The handy reference pages show students how to figure the range, mean, median, and mode of survey data and also how to figure percentages of a population. Students will use it as they analyze the data from their classroom survey.

Step 9: Students are now ready to start finding evidence to support their opinions for their debate. Reproduce and distribute **Researching Your Topics** (page 67). The forms will help students take notes while doing their research on the Internet. Students should use one of these sheets for EACH web site they use as an information source.

Step 10: In most cases students will look ONLY at information that supports their argument. Tell students that in a debate their opponents will try to prove their contentions or reasons are wrong. They must read any research that tries to disprove their contention. Reproduce and distribute **Researching Their Counterarguments** (page 68). Tell students to use this form to list any arguments and evidence the opposing side will use against them.

Note: The research process may last one to two weeks. Feel free to take breaks from student research time by interspersing lessons on **Learning to Think Critically**.

LEARNING THE LANGUAGE OF RESEARCH

Using a Word Wall to Learn Academic Terms

1. Begin teaching the academic terms for debate on a Monday. Write each of these terms on a large sheet of construction paper and tape them up on the wall. (If you feel this is too many terms for your students at once, then just cover half the words the first week and the other half the second week.) Simplified definitions of the terms are provided at the bottom of the page.

2. At the beginning of Monday's class, distribute the record sheet *Learning the Language of Research* (page 48). Don't define the words in the order on the page. Instead, choose the simplest word on the wall that you think most of your students will know. Ask if anyone can define that word. Get as many definitions as you can from your students. Then decide on one simple definition that *everyone* understands. As you write this definition on the board, have students record it in on their forms. Continue until all the words are defined. If no student knows the definition of a word, speak aloud sentences with clear context clues until the students can guess the definition. For example, *My dad collected data about the number of cars speeding on our street and sent it in a report to the mayor. What is data?* Use the practice pages (pages 49 and 50) to help you with context clue sentences.

3. At the beginning of Tuesday's class, tell students to get out a blank sheet of paper and write the numbers 1 to 14 down the left side of the page. Again, begin with the simplest word. Referring to the definitions created Monday, ask students to "Write down the word that means . . ." and read the definition of the simplest word. Students are NOT allowed to look at their definitions. Ask them how they did at the end and then continue your lesson.

4. On Wednesday repeat Tuesday's procedure of calling out the definitions and having students find the correct word on the wall and write it down. However, call out the definitions in a different order. Distribute the **Practice 1** (page 49) and have students complete it.

5. On Thursday repeat Wednesday's procedure of calling out the definitions and having students find the correct word on the wall and write it down. Call out the definitions in another, different order. Distribute the crossword puzzle (page 50) and have students complete it.

6. On Friday repeat Thursday's procedure of calling out the definitions and having students find the correct word on the wall and write it down. Call out the definitions in yet another order. Tell students that this is their test and that the grades count.

Simplified Definitions of Terms:

1. URL – a web address
2. data – information that is collected
3. population – a total number of people in a group
4. questionnaire – a list of questions
5. survey – to ask a group of people the same questions
6. sample – a small part of a larger population
7. mean – the answer that results after adding all the numbers and dividing by the number of numbers
8. median – the number in the middle of a group of numbers
9. mode – the number that occurs the most often
10. percentage – part or all of a group
11. range – the difference between the lowest and highest points in a group
12. search engine – a web site that looks through millions of files for something
13. statistics – facts in the form of numbers
14. generalize – to make a guess based on a small amount of information

Name: _____

Learning the Language of Research

TERM   **DEFINITION**

1. URL   _____
                _____

2. data   _____
                _____

3. population   _____
                _____

4. questionnaire _____
                _____

5. survey   _____
                _____

6. sample   _____
                _____

7. mean   _____
                _____

8. median   _____
                _____

9. mode   _____
                _____

10. percentage _____
                _____

11. range   _____
                _____

12. search engine _____
                _____

13. statistics _____
                _____

14. generalize _____
                _____

Learning the Language of Research

DIRECTIONS: Read each sentence below. The underlined words give a definition or example for one of the vocabulary words. Write that word in the blank provided.

1. _____ You must be very accurate when you type in a web address.

2. _____ The difference between the lowest point and the highest point in the test scores was 33 points.

3. _____ By adding up all the scores and dividing by the total number, David found the average score for the group.

4. _____ The total group of people in the ninth grade is 247 students.

5. _____ The scientists had collected information from our teachers.

6. _____ Google is a web site that looks through millions of files to find something you are interested in.

7. _____ My sister filled out a list of questions about her favorite classes.

8. _____ The mayor used facts in the form of numbers to report daily car thefts.

9. _____ Juan found that only a fraction of the total class liked baseball.

10. _____ When our coach asked us to stand in a line, I was in the exact middle.

11. _____ The number that came up the most often when we guessed our teacher's age was 34.

12. _____ Jessica decided to ask the same set of questions to a group of people to see how many watched "American Idol."

13. _____ Based on Jessica's information that 80 percent of the class watched the show, she could make a guess about the entire group that we liked it.

14. _____ Wanda did not want to ask all ninth graders; she just wanted to ask a small group of the total population.

Name: _____

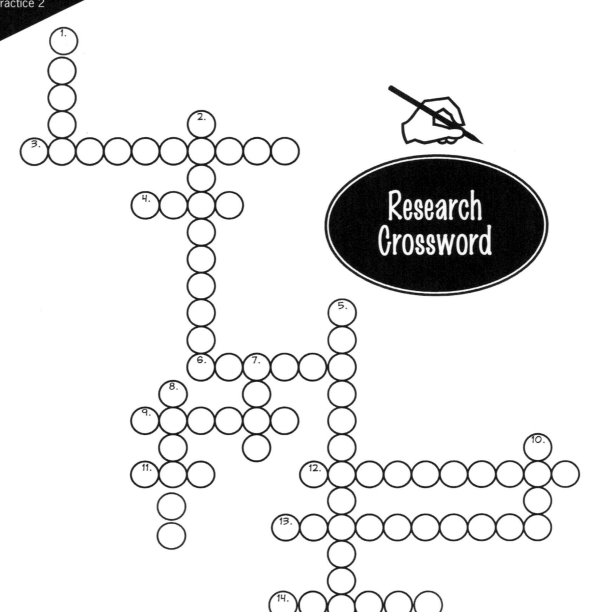

Research Crossword

Across
3. a number representing part or all of a group
4. information that is collected
6. a small part of a larger group
9. the number in the middle of the group
11. a web address
12. the total number of people in a group
13. to make a guess about a large group based on limited information
14. to ask a group of people the same set of questions

Down
1. the difference between the lowest and highest points in a group
2. facts in the form of numbers
5. a list of questions
7. add all numbers and divide by the number of numbers to get this
8. a web site that looks through millions of computer files: _____ engine
10. the number that appears the most often

Using Online Reference Sites

Now that you've chosen a topic, you and your partner will begin to do research to build your argument so that you can WIN your debate. Where will you look for information? You could go to your Library or Media Center and look up your subject in encyclopedias and other reference books. However, since these books may have been printed over a year ago, it is possible that the information is not up to date. You can also find many of these same resources online. Here is a list of major online reference books. If the word "subscription" follows the URL, then you must pay to use this site.

www.encyclopedia.com — Encyclopedia.com provides users with more than 57,000 frequently updated articles from the Columbia Encyclopedia. Each article is enhanced with links to newspaper and magazine articles as well as pictures and maps.

www.encarta.msn.com — Search more than 4,500 articles subdivided into the following categories: Art, Language, and Literature; Life Science; History; Geography; Religion and Philosophy; Physical Science and Technology; Social Science; Sports, Hobbies, and Pets; and Performing Arts.

www.inforplease.com/encyclopedia — This site also provides more than 57,000 frequently updated articles from the Columbia Encyclopedia, subdivided into the following categories: Earth and Environment; History; Literature and Arts; Medicine; People; Philosophy and Religion; Places; Plants and Animals; Science and Technology; Social Sciences and Law; and Sports and Everyday Life.

www.m-w.com — The Merriam-Webster Dictionary is online, and besides providing thousands of definitions, the site also has a Daily Crossword puzzle, a Daily Buzzword game, a Learner's Word of the Day, and for those learning English, a Daily Podcast.

www.bartleby.com — Bartleby is a publisher of literature and reference works. This all-inclusive site has the Columbia online encyclopedia, the American Heritage Dictionary, Roget's II Thesaurus, Columbia Book of Quotations, Bartlett's Familiar Quotations, the Oxford Shakespeare, the King James Bible, Gray's Anatomy, the World Factbook, and Strunk's Elements of Style.

www.factmonster.com — An excellent site for students aged six to fifteen, this site provides Almanac and Feature articles as well as Encyclopedia and Dictionary entries. The site also provides fun trivia and word games.

www.wikipedia.org — Wikipedia is an on-line encyclopedia that is both good news and bad news. The good news is that anyone can edit an article on this encyclopedia. Because things change so quickly in today's world, information can be constantly updated. Also, the articles are free content so that they may be reproduced freely without special permission.
    The bad news is that anyone can edit an article on this encyclopedia! Hence it is possible for someone to post incorrect information about a topic. Wikipedia claims that because so many people are reading the articles, most incorrect information is corrected quickly. If you use Wikipedia for information, be sure to click on the "Page history" link to discover who is responsible for the most recent version and if errors in the article have been spotted by others.

Other reference sites that require a subscription include:
    www.britannica.com and **www.worldbookonline.com**

Using Online Reference Sites
Page 2

Look up your debate topic at Wikipedia, Fact Monster, Bartleby, and at least one other site. If you can't find your topic in one site, then choose another site.

Which of these sites seems to be the most helpful for finding information for your debate?

_____

_____

_____

Explain what you found that is so helpful.

_____

_____

_____

_____

_____

_____

_____

_____

_____

_____

_____

_____

_____

_____

_____

_____

Researching with Search Engines

Reference works like encyclopedias give lots of general information on a topic. You will also want to find current magazine and journal articles that have more up-to-date information. To find the most current information, you'll need to do a more intensive search of the Internet.

1. **Choose Key Words about Your Subject.** Ask yourself what the most important words related to your subject are and use these as you begin your search. In the following examples, possible key words are printed in bold.

   The financial **cost** of the **Iraq war** is not worth the expense.

   Global warming can be solved with **alternative energy** sources.

2. **Think about Organizations or Groups Related to Your Topic.** For example, with global warming, you might consider the **National Academy of Sciences**, the **United Nations**, **Greenpeace**, etc. Look on their web sites.

3. **Start Your Search Engines.** You have probably looked things up on Google or Yahoo. These are search engines. Search engines are computer programs that look through thousands of files to find the key words you type in. The problem with these web sites is that they take you to ANY related information. The site you visit may have accurate information or it may contain incorrect information. For example, let's imagine your topic is the White House. If you are on a computer, type in "White House" on Google. You probably get the following site at the top:

   The White House   www.**whitehouse**.gov/

   Official site. Features a virtual historical tour, history of American presidents and their families, and selected exhibits of art in the **White House**.

   This may be a reliable site since it says "Official site" at the beginning. You need to check the site to be sure. Now look at the third site listed on Google.

   Whitehouse.org   www.**whitehouse**.org/

   Parody of official **White House** web site. Includes spoof news and gossip.

   If you do not read the statement under the URL www.whitehouse.org/ or if you don't know the meaning of the words "parody" or "spoof," you may not realize that everything on this site is fake and meant to make fun of the White House.

   It's okay to search on sites such as Google and Yahoo, but read the information very closely to make sure it's fair and accurate.

4. **Use more than one Search Engine.** While Yahoo and Google are good places to start, you will want to use other search engines to do serious research. One such search engine is Alta Vista at www.altavista.com/. Two other good search engines that have the same feature are Excite at http://excite.com/ and WebCrawler at http://webcrawler.com/.

> Go to www.altavista.com/ now and type the words "White House" into the blank box in front of the word "Find." Hit the Find button. What comes up on your screen? Because search engines often order items by how often they are visited, you may see that "Shop eBay" and "Shopzilla" are listed before a site that refers to the building in Washington, D.C.
>
> Click on the first site that actually is about the building in Washington, D.C. Now look across the top of this web page. What do you see?

5. **Watch Your Punctuation.** If you want to find EVERYTHING about **planets**, then type it in lower case, or all small letters. However, in some search engines, if you type in **<u>Planets</u>**, you'll get only responses with a capital letter.

6. **Narrow Your Search.** What if you are really interested in the White House during the War of 1812? All three of the search engines just mentioned, Alta Vista, Excite, and WebCrawler, use a grouping search called **Boolean Searching**. This is quite a helpful tool and very simple to use. For example, to find information on the San Francisco Giants baseball team and Barry Bonds, type in the following in the Alta Vista search box:

"SF Giants" AND "Barry Bonds"

Now you'll see a list of articles, images, etc., about Barry Bonds who plays for the San Francisco Giants. Here are the different Boolean Searches. Be sure to type the AND, OR, and AND NOT in all capital letters.

To combine 2 or more topics: "hamburgers" AND "hotdogs" AND "French fries"

To limit a topic: "hamburgers" AND "hotdogs" AND NOT "French fries"

To widen a search: "hamburgers" OR "hotdogs" AND "French Fries"

7. **Narrow Your Search Some More.** Another way to limit your search is to use the plus (+) and (–) signs. If there is a term in your search that you MUST have, then put a + sign directly in front of the term without a space. For example, keyboard the following in the Alta Vista search box:

SF Giants AND Barry Bonds, +70th home run

Now all sites this search engine finds will refer to Barry hitting his 70th home run.

You can also stop connections a search engine might make. Suppose you are researching "Barry Bonds" but you are not interested in the controversy about whether or not he took steroids to make him a better hitter. To limit your search, include a minus (–) sign. For example, type in the following in the Alta Vista search box:

SF Giants AND Barry Bonds, –steroids

Now the search engine will leave out, or omit, any articles that mention steroids.

8. **Set up an Alert.** Once you've discovered the best key words for finding your information, some search engines allow you to set an "alert." Google, for instance, allows you to set a "Google Alert" for your subject. Each day you will receive a variety of current articles from many difference sources and perspectives sent to you email. You'll learn how to evaluate these different sources later.

Name: _____

Practicing Boolean Searching

1. **Choose a subject:** First circle the category you want to search below.

Sports   Movie Stars   Fashion   Music

2. **Choose a specific topic:** Write down the specific topic you want to search in your category. For example: Sports: Michael Jordan; Movie Stars: Angelina Jolie; Fashion: Armani; Music: Dr. Dre.

   Your specific topic: _____

3. **Choose a search engine:** Choose either http://www.altavista.com/, http://excite.com/, or http://webcrawler.com/ as your search engine. Open the URL and type in your topic. Fill out the following:

   Specific Topic: _____ # of Responses: _____

   URL of your favorite article: _____

   Title of Article: _____

4. **Narrow Your Search:** Think of a second term and add it to your first topic with an AND. For example: Michael Jordan AND Championships.

   New Topic: _____ AND _____ # of Responses: _____

   URL of your favorite article: _____

   Title of Article: _____

5. **Narrow Your Search More:** Think of a third term that will eliminate some responses. For example: Michael Jordan AND Championships, +1982.

   New Topic: _____ AND _____ # of Responses: _____

   URL of your favorite article: _____

   Title of Article: _____

Name: _____

Evaluating a Web Site

1. **What Site Is This?** Use the URL to find out information. Begin by looking at the ending to the URL, or uniform record locator. Ask yourself what domain, or type of site, gives you the most trustworthy information. Sites that end in **.edu** and **.gov** may be most trustworthy because they are created to share information. Sites ending in **.com** may be less accurate because these are created by companies to sell things. The chart below shows you the most common types of sites.

URL ending	Type of domain or source of site	Example
.com	a company trying to sell something	http://www.amazon.com/
.edu	a school, community college, or university	http://www.unc.edu/
.gov	a local, state, or national government institution	http://www.usa.gov/
.info	an organization that provides information	http://www.microbes.info/
.mil	a military organization	http://www.army.mil/
.net	an internet network source or provider	http://www.ricochet.net/
.org	usually a type of not-for-profit organization	http://www.underoneroof.org/

2. **Who Wrote This?** Find out who the author is. Reliable web sites tell you who wrote the information. Be careful that you are not on a **Personal Page** web site. Personal pages are created by individuals who want to express their own views. There are certain clues that you may be on a Personal Page. If you see a person's name in the URL, such as **bmcbride** or the words **people** or **users**, you are probably on a Personal Page. Also, if you see the tilde symbol (~) or the percent sign (%), you may be on a Personal Page. When you find a web site you want to use, ask yourself the following questions to make sure the author is trustworthy:

- What's the name of the author who wrote the information?
- Are there signs that this is a Personal Page?
- Is there a brief biography of the author, or are there any facts about the author's life that show why he or she is considered an expert?
- What's the author's email address, physical address, or phone number?
- Is there information about whom the author works for? For example, if an author works for a company, he or she may provide information that promotes that company and its products.

3. **Who Published This?** Find out which organization created the web site. Organizations or companies create most web sites. Ask yourself these questions to evaluate the organization that created a web site:

- What is the URL ending?
- Is the name of the organization given that sponsors the site?
- What does the site's "About Us" statement or "Home" page say about the organization's purpose?
- Why might this organization want to publish this information?
- What do others say about this organization?

4. **When Did They Write This?** Find out when the information was written. In today's world, information changes constantly. Knowing how old the information is on a web site lets you know how trustworthy the information is. One way to check the history of a site is to use the web site www.archive.org.

> Try this now if you are on a computer. Go to www.archive.org and type in the site www.underoneroof.org. As you can see, the "Wayback Machine" shows you the history of the site by date. If a date has an asterisk (*) by it, that is a date the site was updated. Clicking on different dates will show you how the home page changed over time. Look for any clues that may tell you that the site might have been created by extremist groups of any kind.

If you use any information from a site, record the date you copied it. Again, things change quickly in today's world and what you find today may not be true in a week or month. The reader needs to know when you found your information. Ask yourself these questions:

- What date was the web site created?
- When was the information you want posted?
- Has this information ever been updated or revised?
  Do you think this information is still true or valid?

5. **What Tone Did the Writer Take?** By reading just a small part of a web site, you can tell a lot about its viewpoint. For example, if the text is funny, then the site is probably using humor to make fun of someone or something. Humorous sites are entertaining but may not present accurate information.

6. **What Sites Are Linked to This Site?** You can check how correct or unbiased a site is by checking what sites it is linked to. Any person, organization, or group can choose to link to a site. Checking to see what other organizations are linked to the site you're interested in is a very simple process.

> Imagine you want to see what sites are linked to the International Reading Association at www.reading.org/. Remember our search engine site www.altavista.com? Go to that site, and in the search box type in the following: link:http://www.reading.org. (To check the links to any site, type in **link:** before the URL with no spaces in the search box.) At the top of the page that appears will be the Home page for the IRA. Below it will be listed all the sites that have linked themselves to the IRA. Because reading is such a popular topic, you'll see above the Home page listing that Alta Vista found over 50,000 links.

Remember to ask yourself the following questions when checking your site:

- What sites are linked to the site from which I'm getting my information?
- Does the linked site say something that no other site agrees with?
- Does the linked site reference other printed information such as magazines, journal and newspaper articles, or books?
- Does the linked site take an extreme or radical view?

7. **Overall, How Accurate or Reliable is This Source?** Two different charts are provided for you to evaluate the web sites you visit when doing your research. Choose one of them and use the chart to take notes on each site to help you decide how trustworthy each site is.

Name: _____

Web Site Evaluation Questionnaire

1. What is the URL of your site?	
2. What does the URL ending tell you about your site?	
3. Is there any sign in the URL that this is a Personal Page?	
4. Who's the author?	
5. What's the author or organization's address?	
6. For whom does the author work?	
7. What organization sponsors the site?	
8. Does the Home Page provide any biased or extreme information?	
9. Why does this organization want to publish this information?	
10. On what date was the site created?	
11. On what date was the article you are reading created?	
12. Do you think this information is still valid based on its date?	
13. Is the tone of this site serious, funny, or satirical?	
14. What source does the writer give for his or her information?	
15. Do any linked sites take a biased or extreme view?	
16. Overall, do you trust the information on this site?	

Name: _____

WEB SITE EVALUATION SHEET

Name of URL site	Name of Author	Name of Publisher	Date of Information	Tone Serious or Fun?	Biased or Untrustworthy Links?	Trustworthy Yes or No?

Name: _____

Learning About Surveys

When you're doing research, you may read about surveys done about your topic. A **survey** is a set of questions asked of a specific group of people.

Imagine you are interested in what afterschool activities your classmates like to do. The total **population** you are interested in would be your entire grade. However, this may be too many people to ask. You could also decide to ask just a small part of this group, or a **sample**. In this case your sample might be just the students in your English class. From the information you gather from your sample, you can make guesses, or **generalize**, about the entire population of all your classmates.

People often use the information from surveys to persuade others to believe or do something. Here are the steps for conducting a survey:

Step 1: Identify the reason for your survey. The first step in conducting a survey is to be clear on the main reason you are conducting it. What exactly is it you want to know? How will you use this information? Will you use it to persuade someone? In our example, we want to know what activities other students in your class do when they go home after school.

Step 2: Decide the form of the data, or information, you collect. Will the information be in the form of numbers? Will you be recording people's opinions? In our example for after school activities, you want to know how long people spend on different activities, so you will collect the information in minutes.

Step 3: Identify the population you want to question. Are you going to ask everyone in the school, or just a small sample? Are you going to ask just the students in one class, one grade level, or just males? In our example, you'll just ask students in this class.

Step 4: Decide how you want to gather information. All surveys use some type of questionnaire, or a list of questions. What will your questionnaire look like? Do you want your sample to answer in complete sentences? Such a form gives lots of information IF the responders take the time to fill it out. Or, do you want your sample to answer with a simple "Yes" or "No," with an "Agree" or "Disagree," or on a Scale of 1 through 5 showing how much responders like or don't like something?

Step 5: Decide when and where to conduct the survey. The data you are collecting often determines when and where you should collect it. Is the time of day important? Does the location where you collect the data make a difference on the responses you get? In our case, you'll collect the data after school, and it will be in people's homes.

Step 6: Analyze the data. Once you've conducted the survey, study the results closely. You'll need to make some sort of Tally Sheet where you can collect all the data and present it on one or two pages. Look for patterns in answers. Did a number of people answer the same way? What was the most common response? If possible, create graphs showing how people responded.

Step 7: Write up a report. Give your report a title that tells the reader exactly what you were studying. In the opening paragraph, explain WHY the study was conducted. In the next paragraph, explain HOW the study was conducted, describing the method you used to gather data. In the next paragraph, give the results of your survey. In the final paragraph, summarize your findings and if possible, make generalizations about the larger population based on your information from your small sample. Then create visual aids, such as graphs, charts, PowerPoint presentations, or even video to present your findings.

Assignment 1

DIRECTIONS: With your classmates, complete all five steps outlined on the **Conducting a Survey** page that follows.

Assignment 2

DIRECTIONS: It's time to create your own survey. Follow the steps above to create and conduct a survey about the topic you've chosen to debate. Build your survey so that people respond with Yes/No, Agree/Disagree, rank responses on a scale of 1 to 5, or answer in numbers of some form such as minutes. Keep your target group small (from 10 to 20 people). Make a Tally Sheet to record all of your responses.

Questionnaire Guidelines

When you are writing a questionnaire, follow these guidelines.

- Make the questions specific. Don't use general words like "usually," "a few," and "in the future." Instead, use specific words such as "each day" or "three times."
- Start with easier questions and move to harder ones. This holds the interest of the responder.
- Write your questions in a logical order, or an order that makes sense to the responder. For example, if you are asking about what food people eat at each meal, start with breakfast, then go to lunch, then dinner.
- Give very clear directions about how you want the person answering, or the person writing the answers, to fill out the form.

Name: _____

Conducting a Survey

DIRECTIONS: The chart below has been created to find out what your classmates do after school and before they go to bed. The chart is designed so that a person who responds must guess, or estimate, the time in minutes they spend on each activity.

Step 1: (Normally you would decide the activities to fill in across the top of the chart below. In this activity that task has been done for you.) Use the chart below to record your activities in minutes.

	Watching TV	Talking on the Phone	Eating or Snacking	Doing Homework	Listening to Music	Playing Outdoors	Talking with Family	On the Computer	Shopping
Time in Minutes									

Step 2: As a class, decide what day you will complete your charts at home and what day the information is due back. (Normally you would decide how, when, and where to distribute this survey. Also, you would decide how you were going to get back the filled-in charts. However, in this case, you and your classmates will each fill out the chart.)

Step 3: Make sure all students take their forms home the day assigned for the research. Also make sure all participants understand they are to write the time in minutes that they spend doing each of the listed activities. To keep the data simple, round seconds up or down to the nearest minute.

Step 4: When the forms are returned, make a master Tally Sheet on the board showing the number of minutes for each participant. (See page 63 for a master tally sheet.)

Step 5: Now go to the section titled *Analyzing Your Data* to learn how to analyze your results.

Afterschool Activities Master Tally Sheet

Student's Name	Watching TV	Talking on the Phone	Eating or Snacking	Doing Homework	Listening to Music	Playing Outdoors	Talking with Family	On the Computer	Shopping

Name: _____

Analyzing Your Data

Once you've collected data, or information, you need to study it to understand what you've found out. If your information is in the form of written responses, then look for patterns, or similar responses that are repeated. When you find a response given often, you know that this is something your sample of people agreed on. Also look at the variety of responses. If you don't get the kind of answer you expected, go back and look at your question. It may have been written in a way that the responder misinterpreted.

Most of the research you read will provide numbers or percentages as a form of response. Our survey on Afterschool Activities provided numbers as answers. Numbers allow you, the researcher, to analyze your data in a number of ways. The first statistic we'll use is called the **mean**.

Finding the Mean

To find the mean of a set of numbers, add all the numbers together, then divide this sum by the total number of numbers you added. Let's imagine you got the following times for Watching TV in your survey.

Student's Name	Maria	David	Juan	Kim	Lee	Sara	Leticia	Shaneka	Mark	Teri	Ahmed
Watching TV	48	37	60	23	60	120	0	48	180	145	60

To find the mean, add all numbers:

$48 + 37 + 60 + 23 + 60 + 120 + 0 + 48 + 180 + 145 + 60 = 781$

Then divide by the total number of numbers: $781 \div 11 = 71$ minutes

The mean, or average, time spent watching TV that night by these 11 people was 71 minutes.

Finding the Range

The second way of looking at your information is to see the **range**. The range is the difference between the lowest and the highest figures. In our example of Watching TV, the lowest figure is 0 and the highest is 180. $180 - 0 = 180$. Thus, the range is 180 minutes.

Finding the Median

The **median** is the middle number of a set of numbers. If there is an even number of numbers, then add the two middle numbers together and divide by 2 to find the median. You can see below that in the example, the median is 60.

$$0, 23, 37, 48, 48, \mathbf{60}, 60, 60, 120, 145, 180$$
5 numbers   5 numbers

Finding the Mode

The **mode** is the number that occurs the most often. In our set of numbers, 48 occurs twice but 60 occurs three times, so 60 is the mode.

$$0, 23, 37, 48, 48, 60, 60, 60, 120, 145, 180$$
2   3

This tells us that more people watched TV for 60 minutes than for any other length of time.

Finding Percentages

You have probably heard in sports that a certain basketball player shot 25 percent. What does this number mean? A 100 percent of anything is all of it. To shoot 100 percent the player would have to make every shot he tried. To find the percentage, you divide a number that describes what you're looking at by the total number of occurrences. For example, we are looking at the shots a player makes. Let's say he made 4 shots. Now we divide this number by the total number of shots he took. He took 16 shots.

$$4 \div 16 = .25 \text{ or } 25/100 \text{ or } 25\%$$

Go back to our example of Watching TV. How do we find out what percentage of students watched for 48 minutes? Our total number of people who watched TV for 48 minutes is 2. Our total number of people who watched TV is 11.

$$2 \div 11 = .18 \text{ or } 18\%$$

This means that 18 percent of the group watched TV for 48 minutes.

Now figure out the following:
1. The percentage of people who watched TV for 180 minutes.
2. The percentage of people who watched TV for 60 minutes.
3. The percentage of people who watched TV for 23 minutes.
4. The percentage of people who didn't watch TV.

Name: _____

Assignment 1

DIRECTIONS: Using the numbers from your Tally Sheet, do the following:

1. Find the mean, median, and mode for each of the activities.

2. Find the range of minutes for each activity.

3. Find the highest and lowest percentages for each activity.

Assignment 2

DIRECTIONS: Now go to your Tally Sheet from the survey you created about your own topic of debate and do the following:

1. If you had responders answer in Yes/No or Agree/Disagree, find the mean of Yes's, No's, Agrees, and Disagrees.

2. If you had responders answer in Yes/No or Agree/Disagree, find the mode for each question you asked.

3. If you had responders answer on a scale of 1 to 5, find the mode for each question you asked.

4. If you had your responders answer in some unit of measurement, such as minutes, or times something was done, then find the mean, mode, and median for each question you asked.

5. Finally, see what percentages you can create to explain your data.

Researching Your Topic

You're ready now to start finding evidence to support your opinion in your debate. Use the form below to take notes. Since you'll be doing your research on the Internet, don't forget to write down the URL source of your information. **Use one of these sheets for EACH web site from which you take information.**

What opinion are you trying to support?

_____

_____

_____

_____

What is the URL address?

What facts did you find to support your idea at this source?

_____

_____

_____

_____

What scientific research, surveys, or quotes from experts did you find?

_____

_____

_____

_____

What real-world examples did you find to support your idea?

_____

_____

_____

_____

Name: _____

Researching Their Counterargument

The opposing team is going to find good arguments to support their viewpoint, just as you have. You need to know what they will say against you and be ready. You MUST read any research that is AGAINST your side. **Use one of these sheets for EACH web site where you find information.**

What is their counterargument?

_____
_____
_____
_____

What is the URL address?

What facts did you find to support their claim?

_____
_____
_____
_____
_____

What scientific research, surveys, or quotes from experts did you find?

_____
_____
_____
_____

What real-world examples did you find to support their claim?

_____
_____
_____
_____

PART 3
LEARNING TO
THINK CRITICALLY

FOR THE TEACHER

FOR THE STUDENT

LEARNING TO THINK CRITICALLY

In Learning to Think Critically students will learn about inductive and deductive reasoning, logical fallacies, and persuasive techniques. They will learn how to choose their strongest contentions, how to give the strongest rebuttals, and how to outline their arguments. Paired teams will then hold 20-minute debates on their topics.

Step 1: Begin by teaching the academic vocabulary students will need to know to understand critical thinking. Teacher directions for Word Wall activities with these words are included. Reproduce the record sheet **Learning the Language of Critical Thinking** (page 73) for individual students and have them record their own definitions. Use the two activity pages (pages 74 and 75) to review and practice these definitions.

Step 2: Part of learning to think critically involves knowing how to reason. Reproduce the reference sheet **Understanding Reasoning** (page 76) for individual students. This sheet provides definitions and practice with both inductive and deductive reasoning.

Step 3: Adolescents often lack the skills to see the faults in arguments. **Recognizing Logical Fallacies** (page 77) introduces students to eight common errors made in reasoning or rhetoric.

Step 4: Reproduce the activity pages **Identifying Logical Fallacies** (pages 78 and 79) for more practice in identifying faulty arguments.

Step 5: To be able to argue well, you must be able to persuade your audience. **Understanding Persuasive Techniques** (page 81) introduces students to a dozen of the most common persuasive techniques used by the media.

Step 6: **Identifying Persuasive Techniques** (page 82) provides students with real-world practice in finding and creating these techniques.

Step 7: **Analyzing Bias and Loaded Language** (page 83) shows students how to look for negative and positive connotations of words.

Step 8: Students need practice in identifying the elements of critical thinking they've just learned. **Applying Your Critical Thinking Skills** (pages 84 and 85) has students analyze the essay on "Off-Campus Lunch" that they first evaluated in Part 1. This time they look for logical fallacies, persuasive techniques, and loaded language.

Step 9: At this point in the process, students have chosen a topic to debate and been placed on a team. They have learned how to research their topic, to recognize and avoid weaknesses in argument, and to use persuasive techniques. **Building a Strong Case** (page 86) will explain how to choose the facts that have the best evidence.

Step 10: Students are now ready to outline their offensive plan! Reproduce and distribute **Planning Your Debate Offense** (pages 87 and 88) so that students can list their strongest contentions and the evidence they will use to support them.

Step 11: Research shows that students rarely know how to refute another person's counterargument effectively. **Building a Strong Rebuttal** (page 89) explains weak and strong responses. Students at this point will look at the opposing team's information to predict how they will respond.

Step 12: Reproduce and distribute **Planning Your Debate Defense** (pages 90 and 91). Students will transfer information collected in **Steps 7** and **8** to this form and formulate their final rebuttals. Having done this, the debate teams now have a script they can follow as they debate in front of their classmates.

Step 13: Before the actual debates begin, pass out **Following the Steps of Debate** (page 92) again, so students can remember the sequence of speakers. (Students used this sheet in their initial debate.) After each debate ends, have the class fill out their forms and then vote on a winner. Caution students NOT to vote on how they initially felt about the topic, but to vote for the team that produces the strongest arguments and rebuttals.

Step 14: To keep the rest of the class listening while students are debating, pass out **Taking Notes on a Debate** (page 93) for them to complete. Students will be able to copy the contentions from the board as the team members put them up. Be sure to have students vote at the end of each debate on a winner and have them explain why that team's arguments were the strongest.

> **Important Note:** If the issue is a sensitive one in which a student may feel ostracized about his or her views, take up the **Notes** sheet and tally the votes in secret; then announce the winners.

Step 15: Students need opportunities to self-assess their performance. Distribute the form **Evaluating Your Debate** (page 94) and walk through the definitions and examples of **concessions, qualifications,** and **reservations**. You may want the two teams to sit together as a group to fill out the evaluation and then have them report back to the class for discussion. After this discussion, let the teams debate again in front of the class. The more they rehearse orally, the better their written papers will be.

Guidelines for Holding Successful 20-Minute Debates

1. For the first few debates, select teams that you believe will be successful. Less able students are able to use these teams as models to see what is expected of them. **You may want to let teams debate twice.** The first debate is their rehearsal and the second counts. Students are normally much more articulate the second time. Having two chances also takes some of the pressure off of a one-time performance.

2. Require students to write their four contentions in complete sentences. Check these before students begin. In this way, the class has a complete sentence to copy on their note-taking sheets when each group presents their contentions.

3. So that the audience always knows what the debaters are referring to, require debaters to use the following phrases as they debate:
   "My first contention is . . ."
   "My second contention is . . ."
   "My first counterargument is . . ."
   "My second counterargument is . . ."

4. To insure that students do balanced research, don't tell the groups of four debaters you've chosen to debate each other which group will argue the Affirmative Side and which will argue the Negative Side until the day before the debate.

LEARNING THE LANGUAGE OF CRITICAL THINKING
Using a Word Wall to Learn Academic Terms

1. Begin teaching the academic terms for debate on a Monday. Write each of these terms on a large sheet of construction paper and tape them up on the wall. Simplified definitions are provided at the bottom of this page.

2. At the beginning of Monday's class period, distribute the record sheet *Learning the Language of Critical Thinking* (page 73). Don't define the words in the order they appear on the page. Instead, choose the simplest word on the wall (the one you think most of your students will know). Ask if anyone can define that word. Get as many definitions as you can from your students. Then decide on one simple definition that everyone understands. As you write this definition on the board, have students copy it onto their forms. Continue until all the words are defined. If no student knows the definition of a word, speak aloud sentences with clear context clues until the students can guess the definition. For example, *It is a fallacy to believe you have a great chance of winning money in a big lottery. Your chances are very small. What is a fallacy?*

3. At the beginning of Tuesday's class period, tell students to get out a blank sheet of paper and number from 1 to 15. Again, begin with the simplest word. Referring to the definitions created on Monday, ask students to "Write down the word that means . . ." and read the definition of the simplest word. Students are NOT allowed to look at their definitions. When you have finished the list, ask students how they did and then move on with your lesson.

4. On Wednesday follow Tuesday's procedure of calling out the definitions and having students find the correct word on the wall and write it down. Call out the definitions in a different order. Distribute the **Practice 1** activity sheet (page 74) and have students complete it.

5. On Thursday follow Wednesday's procedure. Call out the definitions, have students find the correct word on the wall and write it down. Call out the definitions in a different order. Distribute the **Practice 2** activity sheet (page 75) and have students complete it.

6. On Friday follow Thursday's procedure of calling out the definitions and having students find the correct word on the wall and write it down. Call out the definitions in a different order, however. This time tell students that this is their test and the grades count.

Simplified Definitions of Terms:

1. persuade – to try to convince someone
2. alternative – a different choice
3. reasoning – thinking and good judgment
4. stereotype – to say that all members of one group are the same
5. inductive – reasoning that puts fact together to make a decision
6. deductive – reasoning that begins with a general statement and looks for support
7. fallacy – something that is not true
8. logical – makes sense and is reasonable
9. illogical – something that doesn't make sense
10. evade – to avoid
11. testimonial – to speak in favor of something
12. slogan – a saying to sell something
13. generalize – to make a guess based on a small amount of information
14. simplify – to reduce hard problems to easy answers
15. analogy – a similarity between two different things

Name: _____

Learning the Language
of Critical Thinking

TERM

DEFINITION

1. persuade

_____

_____

2. alternative

_____

_____

3. reasoning

_____

_____

4. stereotype

_____

_____

5. inductive reasoning

_____

_____

6. deductive reasoning

_____

_____

7. fallacy

_____

_____

8. logical

_____

_____

9. illogical

_____

_____

10. evade

_____

_____

11. testimonial

_____

_____

12. slogan

_____

_____

13. generalize

_____

_____

14. simplify

_____

_____

15. analogy

_____

_____

Learning the Language
of Critical Thinking

DIRECTIONS: Read each sentence below. The underlined words give a definition or example for one of the vocabulary words. Write that word in the blank provided.

1. _____ Ahmed tried to convince his friends to go to the mall.

2. _____ Mr. Thomas said all people are the same who live in France.

3. _____ Our coach didn't give any other choices than turning the paper in today.

4. _____ It just makes sense and is reasonable to wear a coat on a cold day.

5. _____ Terry often takes a little bit of information and makes big judgments.

6. _____ It is not true that spiders can live inside your stomach.

7. _____ Kelley used good judgment and thinking to finish the puzzle.

8. _____ It doesn't make good sense, or is unreasonable, to wear a coat on a hot day.

9. _____ Marty created a smart saying to advertise our car wash.

10. _____ Sheila laid her head on the desk to avoid being called on by the teacher.

11. _____ Aaron likes to reduce hard problems to easy answers that never work.

12. _____ The pro basketball player gave a talk in favor of wearing a certain brand of tennis shoes.

13. _____ The lawyer put together facts, examples, and evidence to decide what to do next.

14. _____ Felicia can see a similarity between two different things.

15. _____ The lawyer came to a conclusion by beginning with a general statement and then looking for examples that supported it.

Critical Thinking Crossword

Across

3. to reduce hard problems
   to easy answers
5. to say all of one group
   are the same
7. to speak in favor of something
10. to avoid doing something
12. makes sense and is reasonable
15. to make a guess based on limited information

Down

1. good judgment and thinking
2. reasoning that begins with a general statement
   and looks for examples to support it
4. to try to convince someone to do something
6. reasoning that puts together facts and evidence to make a decision
8. a saying to sell something
9. a different choice
11. something that doesn't make sense
13. a similarity between two different things
14. something that is not true

Name: _____

Understanding Reasoning

Whenever you try to solve any problem, you are using reasoning. **Reasoning** is the thinking you do to figure out the best way to do something. For example, when a quarterback is looking at the other team's defense, he is reasoning about which play to run to get the most yards. There are two main methods, or ways, to reason.

Type 1: Inductive Reasoning. One way to solve a problem is to use the **inductive method** in which you use facts and examples to decide on a next step, draw a conclusion, or make a correct generalization. To do inductive reasoning, you need evidence. Police detectives use inductive reasoning in many cases, looking at the evidence to guess who may have committed the crime. Here's an example.

Facts or Evidence

- Our volleyball team won only 2 out of 14 games.
- Most of the players said they didn't understand what to do in their positions on the court.
- Our coach never played volleyball in high school or college.

Conclusion

- We need to get a new, experienced volleyball coach.

Type 2: Deductive Reasoning. A second way to solve a problem or convince someone of something is to use the **deductive method**. Sometimes you make a general statement and then look for specific examples that match the general statement. See the example below.

"Politicians who give money to people to vote for them are dishonest."

↓

"Our mayor pays people to vote for him."

↓

"Our mayor is dishonest."

Activity

DIRECTIONS: With a partner, write two dialogues you might use to convince your parents to let you do something they wouldn't normally allow you to do. In the first dialogue use *Inductive Reasoning*. In the second one use *Deductive Reasoning*. Remember that deductive reasoning begins with a general statement, so you'll need to say something about students or parents. Be ready to perform these dialogues in front of your classmates, and they'll decide which type of reasoning you and your partner used.

Recognizing Logical Fallacies

Have you ever made a good point in an argument only to have the person you are arguing with suddenly say in response, "You're stupid!"? That is a logical fallacy. A logical fallacy occurs when a person uses incorrect reasoning; he or she says something that doesn't answer what you said. There are three main ways a person can evade or ignore an argument:

Type 1: Avoid the Issue

- When someone calls you "stupid" instead of responding to your argument, he or she has dodged, or avoided, the issue or topic. The Latin name for **name-calling** in an argument is **ad hominem**.

- Another way to avoid the issue is to use **circular reasoning**. When people use circular reasoning, they say the same thing they have already said but use different words. Circular reasoning is also called **begging the question**. Here's an example of circular reasoning.

  "Hats in schools should be prohibited
  because hats are not allowed in schools."

- A third way to dodge the issue is to give reasons that don't actually support the main idea being argued. This is called **evading the issue**. Here is an example. Notice that the speaker is not saying why the football coach should be replaced.

  "Our football coach should be replaced.
  Our baseball coach is great."

Type 2: Omit Key Points

- People often omit, or leave out, key ideas when making an argument. One way they do this is to make an **oversimplification**. Here's an example. Notice how other things that cause weight gain are left out.

  "Fast-food restaurants are the cause of overweight people in America."

- Another way to omit key points is to make an **overgeneralization**. You can spot an overgeneralization when you see words like *always, totally, completely,* or *never*.

  "My mother <u>never</u> understands me!"

Recognizing Logical Fallacies
Page 2

Type 3: Ignore Other Alternatives

- People who argue a point may not present all the options. They simply give you an **either/or** choice, or just two choices, leaving out other possible choices that may solve the problem. Here's an example.

    "You either get your homework done <u>now</u>
    or you won't get it done at all."

- Another way to ignore possible solutions is to use a **slippery-slope** argument. This argument suggests that one thing WILL lead to something else, when in reality it may not. Here's an example. Notice that giving Adam a brownie will not lead to giving the rest of the kids anything they want.

    "If I let Adam eat a brownie, I'll have to let your other
    brothers and sisters have anything they want."

- People can also ignore the real cause of something. They may say something causes something when it really doesn't. This is called giving a **false cause**. Here's an example. Notice that the fact that the TV is on didn't cause the tub to overflow.

    "The water overflowed the bathtub
    because the TV was on."

- Sometimes people offer a comparison that doesn't make sense. A comparison between two things is an **analogy**, so they offer a **false analogy.** Here's an example. Notice that teenagers *are* able to make up their minds, so the analogy doesn't work.

    "My father can't make up his mind.
    He's like a teenager."

- Finally, people may use an "expert" to prove their point. However, the expert is NOT an expert in the topic being discussed. This type of logical fallacy is called using a **false authority**. Here's an example. Notice that Rufus Rockhead is an expert in geology, the study of rocks and the earth, not whales or the oceans.

    "Japan's killing of whales makes the ocean cleaner,"
    reported Rufus Rockhead, Ph.D. in Geology.

If They Can Argue Well, They Can Write Well
Copyright ©2008 by Incentive Publications, Inc., Nashville, TN

Identifying
Logical Fallacies

DIRECTIONS: Use the **Learning About Logical Fallacies** reference sheet to figure out which technique is used in each of these statements. Write the fallacy in the blank.

1. Sixteen-year-olds should vote because they're mature, and mature kids should be able to vote.

   _____

2. Greed is the cause of every problem in the world.

   _____

3. You're an idiot if you think that we have the best football team.

   _____

4. A bathtub is like a waterfall in the way it wastes water.

   _____

5. Either we stop depending on foreign oil, or the country will fall apart.

   _____

6. Our politicians are always right when they spend money for local improvements.

   _____

7. Rap music needs to be banned because it's bad. Classical music is good for us, however.

   _____

8. Antoine's dad made him stay home; therefore, we lost the game.

   _____

9. Dr. Laura Pediful, a foot doctor, said gay people should not be allowed to marry.

   _____

10. If the basketball team loses this game, they'll probably lose the rest of their games this season.

    _____

Assignment

DIRECTIONS: With a partner, create a video of an interview with a politician and a reporter. In the interview, one of you as the politician will use **four or more** examples of logical fallacies. Using the **Noting Logical Fallacies** chart, fill in the quotes by the politician so that you can keep track of which fallacies you've used. Digitally record your interview to play for your classmates. Stop the video when a fallacy has been stated. Ask your classmates to identify the fallacy.

Name: _____

Noting
Logical Fallacies

Logical Fallacy	Statement by Politician
Name calling (ad hominem)	
Circular reasoning	
Evading the issue	
Oversimplification	
Overgeneralization	
Either/or	
Slippery Slope	
False cause	
False analogy	
False authority	

Understanding
Persuasive Techniques

People try to persuade you to do things all day long. Your parents persuade you to get up and get dressed for school. Your teachers persuade you to do schoolwork. And the media spends millions of dollars to persuade you to buy certain products. Even *you* try to persuade friends and relatives to do things you wish them to.

Here are some techniques, or ways, people try to persuade someone to do something.

Persuasive Technique	How It Works	Intended Effect
bandwagon	the ad says that everyone else is buying this product or is for this person	to make a person feel left out if they don't do what others do
humor	the ad presents a comic message that creates laughter in the consumer	to make the consumer associate good feelings with the product
individuality	the ad says that people who believe in themselves will like this product or person	to make the person feel self-secure in following his or her own beliefs
name-calling	the ad uses negative images and words to demean another product or person	to make the consumer dislike the other product or person
plain folks	the ad says that good, simple, ordinary people like this product or person	intended for consumers who want a simple product or person
product comparison	the ad compares the benefits of one product or person to another	to show how one product or person is better
purr words	the ad uses words and phrases that produce positive thoughts	to make the product desirable by appealing to the emotions
rewards	the ad promises emotional, physical, financial, or psychological benefits for choosing the product or person	to make the audience want the reward as much as the product or person
security (fear)	the ad uses words and images that make the consumer feel safer with a product or person	to make the audience be fearful to choose the other product or person
slogan	the ad uses a "catchy" phrase that the sticks in the consumer's mind	to keep the product or person in the mind of the consumer
testimonial (celebrity endorsement)	the ad uses a famous person, such as an actor or sports star, to promote the product or person	to impress the audience that someone important chooses the product or person
transfer (emotional appeal)	the ad makes the consumer feel emotions or desire to be happy, sad, athletic, comfortable, or sexy.	to make the audience transfer or associate strong emotions to the product or person

Name: _____

Identifying
Persuasive Techniques

DIRECTIONS: Use the chart on persuasive techniques to figure out which technique is used in each statement. Write the technique in the blank.

1. Everybody is buying a Ford. Shouldn't you? _____

2. You'll feel like a superathlete when you wear the Xtreme Training shoe. _____

3. Rocket clothing is superior to Adonis clothing because of the better material and craftsmanship. _____

4. Only a person who's behind the times would buy a slow, old-fashioned computer from Acme Computers. _____

5. You'll get lots of job offers and make lots of money when you use Rollins employment services. _____

6. If you're an independent, self-confident woman, you won't follow the crowd—you'll buy a Tony watch instead. _____

7. If Michael Jordan says buy Nike, then it's good enough for me. _____

8. Why did the chicken cross the road? To lay it on the line, which is what our lawyers do at Woods, Inc. _____

9. You and your family are open to robbers unless you secure your house with a Magnum Security System. _____

10. The sweet smells of chocolate, the fresh fragrance of baked bread, the scent of cinnamon are at Ed's Bakery. _____

11. Plain people who work hard for a living like in the old days love the value and flavor of Old Time Corn Meal. _____

12. "Stay Cool with Carl's" refrigeration systems. _____

Assignment

DIRECTIONS: Find advertisements in magazines that are examples of at least eight different persuasive techniques. Make either a poster or PowerPoint presentation of these ads for your classmates. Or, create a video commercial that uses four techniques.

Analyzing Bias
and Loaded Language

A **bias** is a preference. If you prefer living in a city to living on a farm, you have a bias towards city, or urban, life.

Writers often share their biases. They may use words to try to persuade the reader to believe as they do. One way writers try to persuade others is to use **stacked facts**. These are facts that support only one point of view. The writer doesn't give opposing ideas.

Another way writers show their biases is to use **loaded language**. When writers add strongly emotional words, often in place of facts, they are trying to use the readers' emotions to feel as they do.

Look at the pairs of words in the chart below. Notice how the word on the left has a positive feeling or meaning, and the word on the right has a negative or bad sense.

Positive	Negative
determined	stubborn
thrifty	cheap
leader	boss
relaxed	lazy
plan	scheme
smart	nerd
athlete	jock

DIRECTIONS: Read some editorials in your newspaper. First look for the use of **stacked facts**. Then list eight words or phrases that are examples of **loaded language**.

Loaded Language examples:

1. _____

2. _____

3. _____

4. _____

5. _____

6. _____

7. _____

8. _____

Name: _____

Applying Your Critical Thinking Skills

Record Sheet

DIRECTIONS: Read the student persuasive essay that follows. The writer of this essay used a number of logical fallacies, persuasive techniques, and loaded words. Use this sheet to record examples used in the essay.

Logical Fallacies:

1. _____
    _____
2. _____
    _____
3. _____
    _____
4. _____
    _____

Persuasive Techniques:

1. _____   2. _____
3. _____   4. _____
5. _____   6. _____

Loaded Language:

1. _____   2. _____
3. _____   4. _____
5. _____   6. _____
7. _____   8. _____

If They Can Argue Well, They Can Write Well
Copyright ©2008 by Incentive Publications, Inc., Nashville, TN

Applying Your Critical Thinking Skills

Persuasive Essay

DIRECTIONS: Use your notes on logical fallacies, persuasive techniques, and loaded language to identify examples in the essay below.

Let's Get Out and Eat Out!
A Persuasive Paper on Off-Campus Lunch

Imagine sitting in the same loud location eating the same kind of foul food for four years of your life. That's what it's like at our high school. We are not allowed to go off campus for lunch. There are a lot of reasons we should have off-campus privileges at lunchtime. We would get better quality food. We would get a break from our teachers, and we would have more time. Also, if we didn't have to eat junk for food, our students would be happier and do better work.

The quality of the food in the cafeteria is bad. No one really likes eating the food there. Most feel it tastes like newspaper. There is just no flavor to anything, unless you consider a lot of salt as flavor. Mr. Jackson, an English teacher, said the food there is not good for us. If we could go to nearby restaurants we could get real food. For example, McDonald's and Taco Bell are right across the street with better tasting food. You can smell the glorious grilling of beef in our halls.

Another reason we should be allowed to go off campus is to get a break from our teachers. When someone is having a bad day, it's good to get away for a while. Even a break of 20 minutes can improve your mood. This break isn't just good for the students. I bet the teachers would like a break from us too, especially since they wouldn't have to do lunch duty where they just yell at kids.

The last reason we need an off-campus lunch is to have more time to eat. Some principals will say it would take too long for us to eat off campus. They think if students go to restaurants no one will ever eat in the cafeteria again and people will lose their jobs. So, most of our lunch time is spent standing in a huge line. By the time we get our food, we have to shove it down in order to get to the next class. If we had off-campus lunch, less people would be in line at any one place.

Why can't students eat hot, moist burgers or spicy tacos instead of putrid peas? Students would get a break from their teachers. We'd have time to relax and digest our food. Come on, everyone. Tell the administration. I say, "Let's get out and eat out!"

Name: _____

Building a Strong Case

You're now going to start selecting your best arguments to build the strongest case you can. During the debate, you will only have time to make a few contentions, or claims, so you must select the best evidence. You will find lots of information while researching.

Follow these three guidelines to select the best evidence.

1. The best evidence has the **3 Rs—right, recent,** and **reliable. Right** means that the information is honest and correct. **Recent** means that the information was collected lately, in the past few years. **Reliable** means that you find the same evidence in more than one source. Other people have come to the same conclusion as your source.

2. The best evidence is <u>directly connected</u> to the issue. Evidence that can be shown to **cause** the proposition is the strongest. Look at these examples about how the death penalty hurts people:

Proposition: The death penalty is cruel and unusual punishment.

Weak Evidence:
"The death penalty is wrong because I don't believe in revenge like 'an eye for an eye.'"
Why it's weak:
The evidence doesn't say anything about the death penalty being cruel and unusual. The evidence is just a personal opinion about revenge.

Strong Evidence:
"The death penalty is wrong because scientists have shown that people being executed go through horrible pain for at least 20 minutes when given the shot to kill them."
Why it's strong:
The evidence shows that the punishment is cruel because it's done with a painful poison that causes a slow death. The evidence gives a scientific fact.

3. If you give an **opinion** instead of a fact as evidence, make sure the opinion is supported with good evidence or examples. Here's an example.

Strong Opinion:
It's my opinion that the death penalty is "unusual" because America is the only civilized western country that uses it. It's unusual that we are the only ones doing it.

Name: _____

Planning Your Debate Offense

DIRECTIONS: You're now about to debate the topic you chose in front of your classmates. Use the page below to note your first two contentions or claims. Your strongest contentions have the best evidence. On the chart below, note the support you have found for each contention or reason.

Your 1st Contention or Claim:

Evidence (facts, research, statistics, surveys, real-world examples) to support this point:

_____

_____

_____

_____

_____

_____

Your 2nd Contention or Claim:

Evidence (facts, research, statistics, surveys, real-world examples) to support this point:

_____

_____

_____

_____

_____

_____

Planning Your Debate Offense
Page 2

DIRECTIONS: Use the page below to note your third and fourth contentions and the evidence you will use to support them.

Your 3rd Contention or Claim:

Evidence (facts, research, statistics, surveys, real-world examples) to support this point:

_____

_____

_____

_____

_____

_____

Your 4th Contention or Claim:

Evidence (facts, research, statistics, surveys, real-world examples) to support this point:

_____

_____

_____

_____

_____

_____

Name: _____

Building a Strong Rebuttal

Most coaches will tell you that it's DEFENSE that wins games. A good defense studies the other team's offense. To win a debate, you need to study the information your debate opponent will use against you. By predicting what they will say, you can be ready with **rebuttals**, or answers to their counterarguments. However, you must LISTEN carefully to what the other team states and answer strongly. There are three types of rebuttals people make in a debate. Do you see why the third is the strongest?

Type 1: Weakest
You simply disagree with your opponent:

Example: "I don't agree that the death penalty is correct."

Type 2: Stronger
You offer an alternative to your opponent's point.

Example: "You said the death penalty is brutal. Well, hanging someone is brutal but death by injection is quick and painless and that's how we do it now."

Type 3: Strongest
You provide evidence that proves the opponent's claim is false or wrong.

Example: "You said that death penalty trials and executions cost a lot, but keeping criminals in prison for life can cost over $19,000 every year they live."

Assignment

DIRECTIONS: As you found research to support your side of the topic, you probably also found research that supports the other side. Now is the time to find more of the opponent's research and read it carefully. Knowing what they may say helps you plan rebuttals. Below, list the strongest points that you think your opponent will make against you. You'll use these points in the next step—**Planning Your Debate Defense**.

1. _____
2. _____
3. _____
4. _____

Name: _____

Planning Your Debate Defense

DIRECTIONS: You're now ready to write out your defensive game plan. Begin by listing your strongest four contentions from **Step 7** on these two pages. Then note possible counterarguments. Finally, based on what you learned in **Step 9**, come up with the **strongest** rebuttals possible. Be sure you don't make any logical fallacies in your arguments.

Your 1st Contention or Supporting Reason:

Their Opposing Views or Counterarguments:

-
-
-
-

Your Rebuttals to Counterarguments:

-
-
-
-

Your 2nd Contention or Supporting Reason:

Their Opposing Views or Counterarguments:

-
-
-
-

Your Rebuttals to Counterarguments:

-
-
-
-

Planning Your Debate Defense
Page 2

DIRECTIONS: Use the page below to note your third and fourth contentions, possible counterarguments to your claims, and how you will answer them. Also, note any **Persuasive Techniques** you want to add in your summary to make it powerful.

Your 3rd Contention or Supporting Reason:

Their Opposing Views or Counterarguments:

-
-
-
-

Your Rebuttals to Counterarguments:

-
-
-
-

Your 4th Contention or Supporting Reason:

Their Opposing Views or Counterarguments:

-
-
-
-

Your Rebuttals to Counterarguments:

-
-
-
-

Name: _____

Following the Steps of Debate

DIRECTIONS: You and your partner are about to debate your topic against another pair of students in front of the class. The chart below shows you the steps the debate will follow. Plan now who will be the 1st speaker and 2nd speaker. Remember to watch for logical fallacies in your opponents' statements. Also, save your strongest points for last and use persuasive techniques in your final summary.

AFFIRMATIVE SIDE

1st Speaker
- States Proposition
- Argues Two Contentions

2nd Speaker
- Records Affirmative Contentions on Board

NEGATIVE SIDE

1st Speaker
- States Any Counterarguments
- Argues Two Contentions

2nd Speaker
- Records Negative Contentions on Board

2nd Speaker
- States Any Counterarguments
- Argues Two New Contentions

1st Speaker
- Records New Affirmative Contentions on Board

2nd Speaker
- States Any Counterarguments
- Argues Two New Contentions

1st Speaker
- Records New Negative Contentions on Board

1st Speaker
- States Any Counterarguments
- Offers Final Rebuttals of all Negative Claims
- Gives Final Persuasive Summary

1st Speaker
- Offers Final Rebuttals of All Affirmative claims
- Gives Final Persuasive Summary

Taking Notes on a Debate

DIRECTIONS: Use this form to take notes on your classmates' debates.

Proposition of Debate: _____

_____

_____

Debaters: Affirmative Side _____   _____

Negative Side _____   _____

Your opinion before the debate: _____

_____

Affirmative Side Contentions and Evidence:	Negative Side Contentions and Evidence:
•	•
•	•
•	•
•	•

Your opinion after the debate: _____

_____

Check whom you think won the debate: Affirmative _____ Negative _____

Name: _____

Evaluating Your Own Debate

DIRECTIONS: In most debates, you learn that both sides have some good or valid claims. Debates show us that it's difficult to say one person's opinion is completely right. Answer these questions to reflect on what you learned during your debate.

1. What strong points did the opposing team make against your argument?

   _____

   _____

   _____

2. When you **concede** something, you admit that a part of what the other team said was correct. What is something that the opposing side said that you might concede or agree with? For example, you might concede that hanging someone to death IS cruel and unusual punishment.

   _____

   _____

   _____

3. In the heat of a debate, you might have used such words as "all," or "never," or "always," or "totally." When you **qualify** a statement, you step back from this extreme view and change the words to "many" or "rarely" or "often" or "nearly always." Think back to the points you made. After listening to the opposing team, write down any **qualifications** you now have about your points.

   _____

   _____

   _____

4. Now that you know the opposing side's claims, you may want to make some **reservations**. Reservations are conditions or situations in which you would be willing to give up your view. For example, after a debate on the death penalty, you might now say, "I stand against the death penalty *except in cases* in which the killer swears he will kill anyone he can get near." What reservations do you now have?

   _____

   _____

   _____

PART 4
LEARNING TO
WRITE PERSUASIVELY

FOR THE TEACHER

FOR THE STUDENT

Teaching Directions

LEARNING TO WRITE PERSUASIVELY

> In Learning to Write Persuasively students will choose a structure for their paper and outline it, learn how to vary their sentences, begin with an interesting opener, learn to paraphrase—not plagiarize, write their draft and use a rubric to revise it, and learn how to cite sources.

Step 1: Begin by teaching the academic vocabulary students will need to know to understand persuasive writing. Step 1 includes directions for how to use Word Wall activities with these words. Reproduce the record sheet **Learning the Language of Writing** (page 98) for individuals to record their definitions. Use the two vocabulary review pages (pages 99 and 100) to review the definitions.

Step 2: Walk students through two different choices for organizing their papers with **Organizing Your Essay** (pages 101–104). Ask them to choose one structure.

Step 3: Now that students have decided on a structure for their paper, have them go back to the notes they took and transfer the information to **Outlining Your Essay** (pages 105–110). They should choose the outline format that matches the structure they chose in Step 2. If they find they have inadequate information to complete the outline, they need to do more research.

Step 4: To help students find a voice and style in their writing, reproduce and distribute the examples in **Varying Your Sentences** (pages 111–113). Students will see examples of sentence openers and closers in the form of phrases and clauses and are provided with practice in these stylistic techniques.

Step 5: Students will also want to begin their papers with a good opener. **Grabbing Your Reader's Attention** (page 114) shows them three effective ways they can begin their papers.

Step 6: Plagiarizing is a difficult problem to stop. **Paraphrasing, Not Plagiarizing** (page 115) explains to students what plagiarism is, and more importantly, how to paraphrase material. Practice in paraphrasing is also provided. If the public domain pieces are too difficult, have students paraphrase material from their textbooks (pages 116 and 117).

Step 7: At this point, students should complete a first draft of their persuasive essay. A rubric for self- and peer review is provided on **Revising Your Paper** (page 118).

Step 8: Finally, students are shown the proper way to cite their sources both within the body of their essay and at the end with **Citing Your Sources** (page 119).

> **Note:** A **Final Grading and Conference Rubric** is provided on page 122. Fill it out, use it as a basis for discussion and revision, and place it in the student's portfolio.

LEARNING THE LANGUAGE OF WRITING
Using a Word Wall to Learn Academic Terms

1. Begin teaching the academic terms for persuasive writing on a Monday. Write each of these terms on a large sheet of construction paper and tape them up on the wall.

2. At the beginning of Monday's class period, distribute *Learning the Language of Writing* (page 98). Don't define the words in the order they appear on the page. Instead, choose the simplest word on the wall (the one that you think most of your students will know). Ask if anyone can define that word. Get as many definitions as you can from your students. Then decide on one simple definition that everyone understands. As you write this definition on the board, have students copy it onto their record sheet. Continue until all the words are defined. If no student knows the definition of a word, speak aloud sentences with clear context clues until the students can guess the definition. For example, *My teacher asked me to cite my sources in my paper, so at the end I listed every source from which I found some material. What does "cite" mean?*

3. At the beginning of Tuesday's class period, tell students to get out a blank sheet of paper and number from 1 to 15. Again, begin with the simplest word. Referring to the definitions created on Monday, ask students to "Write down the word that means . . ." and read the definition of the simplest word. Students are NOT allowed to look at their definitions. When you are finished with all the words, ask students how they did at the end and then move on with your lesson.

4. On Wednesday, follow Tuesday's procedure of calling out the definitions and having students find the correct word on the wall and write it down. Call out the definitions in a different order than you did on Tuesday. Distribute the **Practice 1** activity sheet (page 99) and have students complete it.

5. On Thursday, follow Wednesday's procedure of calling out the definitions and having students find the correct word on the wall and write it down. Call out the definitions in a new different order. Distribute the crossword puzzle (page 100) and have students complete it.

6. On Friday, follow Thursday's procedure of calling out the definitions and having students find the correct word on the wall and write it down. Call out the definitions in yet another order. This time tell students that this is their vocabulary test and that the grades will count.

Simplified Definitions of Terms:

1. essay – short writing of someone's opinion
2. sentence – a group of words that gives a complete thought
3. paragraph – a group of sentences on one topic
4. rhetoric – writing that is persuasive
5. synonym – a word that means almost the same
6. subject – who or what a sentence or study is about
7. clause – a group of words containing a subject and a verb
8. phrase – two or more words together that are not a complete sentence
9. plagiarize – to present someone else's ideas as your own
10. paraphrase – to rewrite in different words
11. cite – to quote as support for something
12. citation – a documentation of the source of information
13. reference – a work often used as a source
14. revise – to change in order to improve
15. rubric – a description of what makes up a good paper

Name: _____

Learning the Language of Writing

TERM	DEFINITION
1. essay	
2. sentence	
3. paragraph	
4. rhetoric	
5. synonym	
6. subject	
7. clause	
8. phrase	
9. plagiarize	
10. paraphrase	
11. cite	
12. citation	
13. reference	
14. revise	
15. rubric	

Name: _____

Learning the Language
of Writing

DIRECTIONS: Read each sentence below. The underlined words give a definition or example for one of the vocabulary words. Write that word in the blank provided.

1. _____ Sean's first group of sentences all focused on one topic—how much the death penalty cost Americans.

2. _____ Dante began his first sentence with the words, "Walking quickly."

3. _____ Our teacher told us to rewrite other people's words into our own.

4. _____ The entire essay was written to persuade us to vote for Jackson.

5. _____ She asked me to choose a word that meant almost the same as "cold."

6. _____ We read an article that gave someone's opinion about cell phones.

7. _____ Sam admitted that he had copied another person's words as his own.

8. _____ The scientists were sure to quote others who supported their research.

9. _____ This is the second time I've had to rewrite the paper to make it better.

10. _____ When I read my sentence aloud, Sara didn't know who or what the sentence was about.

11. _____ Mark wrote down the two sources of information for his report.

12. _____ My brother used the newspaper as a source of information.

13. _____ Mrs. Daniels, our teacher, gave us a description of what is included in a good essay.

14. _____ Jose always wrote his words in complete thoughts.

15. _____ Kim added the words "because she was tired" to the end of her sentence "Jill quit studying."

Name: _____

Writing Crossword

Across

1. two or more words that are not a complete sentence
5. a group of words that give a complete thought
7. a group of words with a subject and a verb
11. work used as a source
13. copying someone else's words without permission

Down

1. group of sentences on one topic
2. to change in order to improve
3. who or what a sentence or study is about
4. short writing of someone's opinions
6. documentation of source information
8. a word that means almost the same as another
9. rewriting someone else's words into your own words
10. writing that is persuasive
12. a description of what makes up good writing

Organizing Your Essay

You're now ready to turn your notes from your debate into a persuasive essay. You have a choice as to how you want to set up, or structure, your paper. Study the two choices that follow and pick the one that makes the most sense for you. Then transfer your notes to the blank graphic organizers of the structure you like in **Step 3**.

Structure 1

Introduction
- Opening sentence that gets the reader's attention
- Statement of your stance on the proposition
- Short summary of your reasons for your opinion

2nd Paragraph
- Your first contention, or reason, for supporting your opinion
- Facts, statistics, or real-world examples that support your statement
- Possible counterarguments to your first contention
- Rebuttals and/or concessions to your first contention

3rd Paragraph
- Your second contention, or reason, for supporting your opinion
- Facts, statistics, or real-world examples that support your statement
- Possible counterarguments to your second contention
- Rebuttals and/or concessions to your second contention

4th Paragraph
- Your third contention, or reason, for supporting your opinion
- Facts, statistics, or real-world examples that support your statement
- Possible counterarguments to your third contention
- Rebuttals and/or concessions to your third contention

5th Paragraph
- Your fourth contention, or reason, for supporting your opinion
- Facts, statistics, or real-world examples that support your statement
- Possible counterarguments to your fourth contention
- Rebuttals and/or concessions to your fourth contention

Conclusion
- Restatement of your opinion
- Brief summary of your support for your opinion
- Restatement of any logical fallacies in opposing arguments and rebuttals
- Closing statements using any appropriate persuasive techniques

Name: _____

Organizing Your Essay

Below is a second way to set up, or structure, your essay. Study this structure, then transfer your notes to the blank graphic organizers of the structure you like in **Step 3**.

Structure 2

Introduction
- Opening sentence that gets the reader's attention
- Statement of your stance on the proposition
- Short summary of your reasons for your opinion

2nd Paragraph
- Your first contention, or reason, for supporting your opinion
- Facts, statistics, or real-world examples that support your statement
- Your second contention, or reason, for supporting your opinion
- Facts, statistics, or real-world examples that support your statement

3rd Paragraph
- Your third contention, or reason, for supporting your opinion.
- Facts, statistics, or real-world examples that support your statement
- Your fourth contention, or reason, for supporting your opinion
- Facts, statistics, or real-world examples that support your statement

4th Paragraph
- Counterarguments to your first contention
- Counterarguments to your second contention
- Counterarguments to your third contention
- Counterarguments to you fourth contention

5th Paragraph
- Rebuttals and/or concessions to your first counterarguments
- Rebuttals and/or concessions to your second counterarguments
- Rebuttals and/or concessions to your third counterarguments
- Rebuttals and/or concessions to your fourth counterarguments

Conclusion
- Restatement of your opinion
- Brief summary of your support for your opinion
- Restatement of any logical fallacies in opposing arguments and rebuttals
- Closing statements using any appropriate persuasive techniques

Outlining Your Essay

Structure 1

DIRECTIONS: Fill out this form to outline your essay. Use notes from your debate and your research. Use key words and phrases instead of complete sentences.

Structure 1 – Page 1

Introduction

Your Opinion on the Topic: _____

_____

Brief Summary of Reasons: _____

_____

_____

_____

_____

2nd Paragraph

1st Contention: _____

_____

Supporting Research: _____

_____

_____

_____

Counterarguments:

-
-
-

Rebuttals:

-
-
-

Name: _____

Outlining Your Essay

Structure 1 – Page 2

3rd Paragraph

2nd Contention: _____
_____

Supporting Research: _____
_____
_____
_____

Counterarguments: Rebuttals:

•   •

•   •

•   •

↓

4th Paragraph

3rd Contention: _____
_____

Supporting Research: _____
_____
_____
_____

Counterarguments: Rebuttals:

•   •

•   •

•   •

Outlining Your Essay

Structure 1 – Page 3

5th Paragraph

4th Contention: _____

_____

Supporting Research: _____

_____

_____

_____

Counterarguments: Rebuttals:

•   •

•   •

•   •

Conclusion

Your Opinion on the Topic: _____

_____

Summary with Emotional Appeal: _____

_____

_____

_____

_____

_____

_____

_____

Name: _____

Outlining Your Essay

Structure 2

DIRECTIONS: Fill out this form to outline your essay. Use notes from your debate and your research. Use key words and phrases instead of complete sentences.

Structure 2 – Page 1

Introduction

Your Opinion on the Topic: _____

_____

Brief Summary of Reasons: _____

_____

_____

_____

_____

2nd Paragraph

1st Contention: _____

_____

Supporting Research: _____

_____

_____

_____

2nd Contention: _____

_____

Supporting Research: _____

_____

_____

_____

Outlining Your Essay

Structure 2 – Page 2

3rd Paragraph

3rd Contention: _____
_____

Supporting Research: _____
_____
_____
_____

4th Contention: _____
_____

Supporting Research: _____
_____
_____
_____

4th Paragraph

Counterarguments to 1st Contention: _____
_____
_____

Counterarguments to 2nd Contention: _____
_____
_____

Counterarguments to 3rd Contention: _____
_____
_____

Counterarguments to 4th Contention: _____
_____
_____

Name: _____

Outlining Your Essay

Structure 2 – Page 3

5th Paragraph

Rebuttal to 1st Counterargument: _____
_____
_____

Rebuttal to 2nd Counterargument: _____
_____
_____

Rebuttal to 3rd Counterargument: _____
_____
_____

Rebuttal to 4th Counterargument: _____
_____
_____

Conclusion

Your Opinion on the Topic: _____
_____

Summary with Emotional Appeal: _____
_____
_____
_____
_____
_____
_____
_____

Varying Your Sentences

DIRECTIONS: Read the following paragraph. What is wrong with the way it is written?

> "I do believe in the death penalty. I think killers should be killed. I think they have hurt others very badly. I think it is horrible that they should live after they kill someone. I believe they should go from the courtroom to the electric chair."

In the above paragraph, the writer uses the same words and type of sentence over and over again. This writer uses a form of the word "kill" three times, "think" three times, and "believe" twice. Also, every sentence begins with the subject "I" and is followed by either the verb "believe" or "think." To make your writing more interesting, you should vary, or change, your words and sentence structures.

Vary your words.

You can find a **synonym**, or word that means nearly the same thing as another word, by looking up your word in a thesaurus or a dictionary. For example, in a thesaurus you will see that a synonym for "killer" is "murderer."

Activity

DIRECTIONS: Write synonyms for the following words in the blanks below.

penalty _____   hurt _____

badly _____   horrible _____

jail _____   crime _____

Vary your sentences with openers.

There are many ways to change a sentence from the simple subject-verb structure to something more interesting. One way is to change the beginning, or opening, of the sentence. Here are five sentence openers.

1. Begin with an adverb.
   For example: **Honestly**, I do believe in the death penalty.

2. Begin with a prepositional phrase.
   For example: **Without any hesitation**, I think that murderers should be killed.

3. Begin with a participle phrase.
   For example: **Having hurt others badly**, they should die for their felonies.

4. Begin with a noun clause, or a group of words that acts as the subject.
   For example: **That they should live when others died** is disgusting.

5. Begin with a clause that tells time.
   For example: **After homicidal maniacs walk out of court**, they should go directly to the
   electric chair.

Notice how much more interesting the opening paragraph sounds now.

> "Honestly, I believe in the death penalty. Without any hesitation, it is my opinion
> that murderers should be executed. Having hurt others badly, they must die for
> their felonies. That they should live when others died is disgusting. After
> homicidal maniacs walk out of court, they should go directly to the electric chair."

Activity

DIRECTIONS: Add the type of sentence opener called for in these sentences.

1. My dog was hit by a car yesterday. *(adverb)*

   _____

2. My brother refused to go inside the haunted, scary house. *(participle phrase)*

   _____

3. It is amazing that you passed the test. *(noun clause)*

   _____

4. The turkey was burning inside the oven. *(prepositional phrase)*

   _____

5. We'll start eating as soon as everyone gets home. *(clause that tells time)*

   _____

If They Can Argue Well, They Can Write Well
Copyright ©2008 by Incentive Publications, Inc., Nashville, TN

Vary your sentences with closers.

Another way to make a sentence more interesting is to change the ending, or closing, of the sentence. You can add phrases or clauses to the ends of sentences. Here are some examples:

Add phrases:

1. Juan was chasing the loose ball. He was running as fast as he could.
   Juan was chasing the loose ball, **running as fast as he could.**

2. Sarah hated the old house. It was a dirty building filled with rats.
   Sarah hated the old house, **a dirty building filled with rats.**

3. Ahmed cried all night. He had lost the game by missing the last shot.
   Ahmed cried all night, **sad that he'd lost the game by missing the last shot.**

Add clauses:

1. Sherry loved sitting next to Carlos. He always smiled when she sat down.
   Sherry loved sitting next to Carlos, **who always smiled when she sat down.**

2. He saw Sarita at the beach. Her brother had once been his friend.
   He saw Sarita at the beach, **whose brother had once been his friend.**

3. I just played tennis. It is one of my favorite things to do.
   I just played tennis, **which is one of my favorite things to do.**

Activity

DIRECTIONS: Add a sentence closer for these sentences.

1. My dog was hit by a car yesterday. He was chasing an old tennis ball.

   _____

2. My brother refused to race Mike. Mike always cheated.

   _____

3. I really love rides at the fair. I'm happy to be scared by them.

   _____

4. Shenika spends the summer swimming. This is something I like to do, too.

   _____

Grabbing Your Reader from the Start

Have you ever noticed that some things you read are boring from the very first sentence? As a writer, you want to grab your readers' attention by saying something witty, humorous, or even shocking.

Look back at the student essay entitled "Let's Eat Out" that you graded in Part 1 of this book. Here's the opening sentence below. How interesting is it?

"We students at school should be allowed to go off campus to eat our lunch, but we are not allowed to."

What if we started in one of these ways instead?

Why are we fed like people in jail? (shock)

Everybody up to the pig trough; it's feeding time! (humor)

"Please Sir, may I have NO more." (witty, based on the novel "Oliver Twist")

Activity

DIRECTIONS: For each topic listed below, write an interesting first sentence. Your classmates should be able to tell if you're using wit, humor, or shock.

1. Everyone must wear school uniforms at school.

   _____

   _____

2. The age to get a driver's license ought to be 18 years old.

   _____

   _____

3. All athletes must make the B honor roll.

   _____

   _____

4. Violent video games should be banned.

   _____

   _____

Paraphrasing, Not Plagiarizing

When you are doing research, you often find information you want to use to support your opinion. If you copy, or "cut and paste," this information from another person's writing and place it in your own paper without citing the source, you have **plagiarized**, or stolen, the other person's work. Plagiarizing is illegal and it can get you suspended or thrown out of many schools and universities. It is easy to spot material that has been plagiarized. Teachers now have computer programs such as *Turnitin* that scan your paper to find parts that have been plagiarized.

You can avoid plagiarizing by paraphrasing instead. To **paraphrase** is to restate, or rewrite, the writer's ideas in your <u>own</u> words. Normally when you paraphrase, you rewrite the original material in a shorter, simpler form. Below is an original piece of text taken from "The Agencies of American Colonization." Read this original piece. Then read the paraphrased version that follows.

Original Text:

It was no light matter for the English to cross three thousand miles of water and found homes in the American wilderness at the opening of the seventeenth century. Ships, tools, and supplies called for huge outlays of money. Stores had to be furnished in quantities sufficient to sustain the life of the settlers until they could gather harvests of their own. Artisans and laborers of skill and industry had to be induced to risk the hazards of the new world. Soldiers were required for defense and mariners for the exploration of inland waters. Leaders of good judgment, adept in managing men, had to be discovered. Altogether such an enterprise demanded capital larger than the ordinary merchant or gentleman could amass and involved risks more imminent than he dared to assume.
(The Project Gutenberg Ebook of History of the United States by Charles A. Beard and Mary R. Beard; Source: www.gutenberg.org/etext/16960)

Now see how a student has paraphrased this same text below.

Paraphrased Text:

Coming to America in the sixteen hundreds was very risky personally and financially for English settlers. Sailors, ships, soldiers, and supplies cost a great deal. If the settlers survived crossing the Atlantic Ocean, they would then have to survive living in the wilderness until they could build farms and raise food.

Activity

DIRECTIONS: List three differences you see between the original text and the paraphrased text that you just read.

1. _____

2. _____

3. _____

Name: _____

Using Exact Quotations

Sometimes you may want to use some of the exact words a writer has used. For example, you might want to copy words or ideas . . .

  . . . that are detailed instructions, dates, or statistics you don't want to get wrong.

  . . . that could be misrepresented or misunderstood if you tried to paraphrase them.

  . . . that are so well written that you want the reader to see the writer's words.

You can copy these words exactly if you put quotation marks around the section of text you copy AND state the source. Note how this writer has used quotation marks and cited his source.

> The Civil War almost destroyed our country. In Abraham Lincoln's *Gettysburg Address*, the president tells us that our country was "conceived in liberty and dedicated to the proposition that all men are created equal." In so doing he reminds all Americans of the guiding principles of our founding fathers.

To paraphrase well, follow these steps.

1. Read the original text until you are sure you understand its meaning. If necessary, look up any unknown words. If the text is hard to understand, ask a friend to read the text and explain it to you in his or her own words.

2. Once you feel you understand the original text, then set it aside and try to summarize, or restate, the main ideas. Remember that a paraphrase is often shorter than the original text. Ask yourself, "What was the main point this person was making?" Write that in your own words.

3. To help you say something similar to the original text, use a thesaurus to find synonyms, or words that mean nearly the same thing as the author's words.

4. Once you've written your paraphrase, place the original text beside your rewrite. Reread both pieces to make sure that you have included all the main ideas in your own words.

5. Don't change important facts, dates, numbers, or statistics. Changing facts would make the text incorrect and unreliable. You may want to copy these and use quotes.

6. If you want to copy something exactly from the author, remember to put quotation marks at the beginning and end of the statement that is copied. The quotation marks tell the reader that these are the author's original words. **Step 8: Citing Your Sources** will show you how to do this.

7. Finally, jot down the source of the author's text, including the page number, printed source or Internet URL, the date of the publication, and the date you found it so that you can properly cite the material in your paper.

Practicing Your Paraphrasing Skills

DIRECTIONS: Choose two of the following six primary sources and rewrite each as a paraphrase. Then choose phrases or ideas which you feel are so well stated that they should be copied exactly, and place quotation marks around that text.

---

1. *from "A Short Account of the History of Mathematics" (4th edition, 1908) by W. W. Rouse Ball:*
   Isaac Newton's father, who had died shortly before Newton was born, was a yeoman farmer, and it was intended that Newton should carry on the paternal farm. He was sent to school at Grantham, where his learning and mechanical proficiency excited some attention. In 1656 he returned home to learn the business of a farmer, but spent most of his time solving problems, making experiments, or devising mechanical models; his mother noticing this, sensibly resolved to find some more congenial occupation for him, and his uncle, having been himself educated at Trinity College, Cambridge, recommended that he should be sent there.
   Source: www.maths.tcd.ie/pub/HistMath/People/Newton/RouseBall/RB_Newton.html

---

2. *from The Adventures of Colonel Daniel Boone:*
   Thus we behold Kentucke, lately an howling wilderness, the habitation of savages and wild beasts, become a fruitful field; this region, so favourably distinguished by nature, now become the habitation of civilization, at a period unparalleled in history, in the midst of a raging war, and under all the disadvantages of emigration to a country so remote from the inhabited parts of the continent.
   Source: http://www.pagebypagebooks.com

---

3. *from the U.S. Constitution Preamble:*
   We the People of the United States, in Order to form a more perfect Union, establish Justice, insure domestic Tranquility, provide for the common defense, promote the general Welfare, and secure the Blessings of Liberty to ourselves and our Posterity, do ordain and establish this Constitution for the United States of America.
   Source: http://caselaw.lp.findlaw.com

---

4. *from The Gettysburg Address, delivered by Abraham Lincoln:*
Four score and seven years ago, our fathers brought forth upon this continent a new nation, conceived in liberty and dedicated to the proposition that all men are created equal. Now we are engaged in a great civil war, testing whether that nation or any nation so conceived and so dedicated can long endure. We are met on a great battlefield of that war. We have come to dedicate a portion of that field as a final resting place for those who here gave their lives that that nation might live. It is altogether fitting and proper that we should do this . . .
Source: http://libertyonline.hypermall.com/Lincoln/gettysburg.html

5. *from "The North Wind and the Sun" (Aesop's Fables):*
The North Wind and the Sun disputed as to which was the most powerful, and agreed that he should be declared the victor who could first strip a wayfaring man of his clothes. The North Wind first tried his power and blew with all his might, but the keener his blasts, the closer the Traveler wrapped his cloak around him, until at last, resigning all hope of victory, the Wind called upon the Sun to see what he could do. The Sun suddenly shone out with all his warmth. The Traveler no sooner felt his genial rays than he took off one garment after another, and at last, fairly overcome with heat, undressed and bathed in a stream that lay in his path. MORAL: Persuasion is better than force.
Source: www.aesopfables.com

6. *from The base of the Statue of Liberty by Emma Lazarus:*
Give me your tired, your poor, Your huddled masses yearning to breathe free, The wretched refuse of your teeming shore. Send these, the homeless, tempest-tost to me, I lift my lamp beside the golden door!
Source: http://Wikipedia.org

Revising Your Paper

When you finish writing the first draft of your paper, use the following rubric, or checklist, to see how well you've done so far. Share your paper with one or two classmates and ask them to read and fill out the form below. When you get the forms back, first look to see what parts you did well. Then look to see where your readers think your work is "poor" or "average." Go back to those lessons and reread them, and then write another draft that strengthens the weaker sections.

Rubric for Evaluation

Name: _____ Date: _____

	Poor	Average	Great
Expression of Ideas			
Grabs the reader's attention at the beginning of the essay.			
Clearly states the issue and the reader's opinion.			
Supplies supporting evidence in the form of facts.			
Supports opinions with research and statistics.			
Supports opinions with quotes from experts.			
Supports opinions with real-world examples or stories.			
Provides appropriate opposing views.			
Provides rebuttals or concessions to opposing views.			
Avoids logical fallacies in the argument.			
Either paraphrases or cites sources and uses quotation marks for copied text.			
Structure			
Uses a clear structure that the reader can follow.			
Uses a variety of sentence structures to hold the reader's interest.			
Ends with a persuasive summary.			
Grammar and Mechanics			
Contains no more than three errors in grammar.			
Contains no more than three errors in spelling, punctuation, and capitalization.			

Name: _____

Citing Your Sources

After you have written your final draft of your paper, you need to show the reader where you found your information. Hopefully you have been writing down all your book and Internet sources. The models below show you the proper style or format for listing your sources on a References page.

Citing a Source within Your Paper

If you decided to copy a section of text from another author or refer to his or her work, you must let the reader know that these are not your original ideas. To show the reader the exact words you have copied, place quotation marks at the beginning and end of the copied text. Then, just before the period, inside parentheses write the author's name and the page or pages from which you took the quote. Here's an example:

> Students who practice debate "tend to be excellent speakers" (Fine, 274).

If you are just referring to research or ideas of another author, but not copying the author's words, then you can simply put the author's last name and the copyright date in parentheses just before the period. The reader can then look at your References at the end of your paper to get all of the information. Here's an example:

> Students should do more debating in their classrooms (Schmoker, 2006).

Providing a Reference Page

At the end of your paper, you will have a page entitled **References** that lists all the sources you used to gather information. These sources are listed in alphabetical order starting with the first letter in the author's last name. If there is more than one author, use the first author listed. Here's the correct MLA format for citing your sources:

Citing Print Materials—Books

Books with one author:

Last Name, First Name. <u>Title of Book</u>. City of publication: Publisher, copyright date.

Example: Fine, Gary. <u>Gifted Tongues: High School Debate and Adolescent Culture.</u> Princeton, NJ: Princeton University Press, 2001.

Books with two or three authors:

Last Name, First Initial; Last Name, First Initial; and Last Name, First Initial. <u>Title of Book.</u> City of Publication: Publisher, copyright date.

Example: Behrens, L., & Rosen, L.J. <u>Writing and reading across the curriculum</u> (6th ed.) New York: Longman. 1997.

Books with many authors:

Last Name, First Name of first or lead author followed by the words *et al.* <u>Title of Book</u>. City of publication: Publisher, copyright date.

Example: Massey, B. *et al.* <u>Butterflies and other insects.</u> San Francisco: Jacobs. 1975.

An edited work with no single author:

Editor's Last Name, First Initial. ed. <u>Title of book</u>. City of Publication: Publisher. copyright date.

Example: Howes, R. G. ed. <u>Historical Studies of Rhetoric and Rhetoricians</u>. Ithaca: Cornell University Press. 1961.

An author in an edited work:

Author's Last Name, First Name. Title of chapter or article. In Editor's First Initial, Last Name (ed.) <u>Title of book</u>. City of Publication: Publisher. copyright date.

Example: Kuhn, D. What is scientific thinking and how does it develop? In U. Goswami (ed.) <u>Handbook of childhood cognitive development</u>. Oxford: Blackwell. 2002.

Citing Print Materials—Newspapers, Journals, or Magazines

Article in a journal, magazine, or newspaper:

Author's Last Name, Initials. "Title of article." <u>Name of journal or magazine</u>, Vol. Number (Year of publication): pages.

Example: Johannessen, L.R. "Teaching thinking and writing for a new century." <u>English Journal</u>, 90.6 (2001): 38–46.

Citing Internet Sources

Professional web site with no author:

<u>Title of Home Page</u>. Date. Name of Organization. Date you found the information <URL>.

Example: <u>Association for Supervision and Curriculum Development Home Page</u>. 2007. ASCD. 3 May 2007 < http://www.ascd.org/portal/site/ascd>

Online magazine with an author:

Last Name, First Initial of author. "Article Title." *Site Name.* Date of article. Organization Name. Date you found the information < URL >.

Example: Winter, R. "Teacher in chief." *Time.* 3 February , 2001, Time Magazine and CNN 5 May, 2007, from <http://www.time.com/time/education/article/0,8599,98013,00.html>

Online journal with an author:

Last Name, First Initial of author. "Article Title" <u>Journal Name</u> Vol. Number (Year): Date you found the information < URL >.

Example: Pressley, M. "Comprehension instruction: What makes sense now, what might make sense soon." <u>Reading Online</u> 5.2 (2002): 5 May 2007 <http://www.readingonline. org/articles/art_index.asp?HREF=/articles/handbook/pressley/index.html>

Web site from a subscription service:

"Title of Article." <u>Name of subscription service</u>. Date you found the information. Search Keyword to find subscription service: and/or <URL>

Example: "Cinco de Mayo." <u>HighBeam Encyclopedia</u>. May 3, 2007. Keyword: HighBeam. <http://www.encyclopedia.com/doc/1B1-360811.html>

Finally, should you ever be confused about the format of a source you are citing, you can also go to the following web site on the Internet. Once at the site, simply type in the information you have, and the site will automatically rearrange it in the correct style, including the correct punctuation. You can find this "citation machine" at <http://citationmachine.net/>.

Final Assignment

DIRECTIONS: Now that you've written your persuasive paper, do something with the information you've learned. Choose one of these ideas or create one of your own:

• Shorten your essay into an editorial for either your school or local newspaper;

• Make a video as a Public Service Message expressing your views to be broadcast over an education channel.

• Conduct a schoolwide survey on your topic to see what your classmates think. Then show a video version of your debate and survey the students again.

Final Grading and Conference Rubric

Student's Name: _____   Date: _____

	Poor	Average	Great	Comments
Expression of Ideas				
Grabs the reader's attention at the beginning of the essay.				
Clearly states the issue and the reader's opinion.				
Supplies supporting evidence in the form of facts.				
Supports opinions with research and statistics.				
Supports opinions with quotes from experts.				
Supports opinions with real-world examples or stories.				
Provides appropriate opposing views.				
Provides rebuttals or concessions to opposing views.				
Avoids logical fallacies in the argument.				
Either paraphrases or cites sources and uses quotation marks for copied text.				
Structure				
Uses a clear structure that the reader can follow.				
Uses a variety of sentence structures to hold the reader's interest.				
Ends with a persuasive summary.				
Grammar and Mechanics				
Contains no more than three errors in grammar.				
Contains no more than three errors in spelling, punctuation, and capitalization.				
Cites sources properly				

ADDITIONAL RESOURCES

Internet Research Resources

Web Tutorials

Instructional Internet – Landmark for Schools

http:// landmark-project.com/page.php?stamp=&pn=8&psn=&cat=30

District 214's Lessons to Explain the Web:

http://www3.dist214.k12.il.us/lesson/index.html

Five Types of Slam Dunk Digital Lessons by Jamie McKenzie

http://fno.org/sum04/fivekinds.html

Boolean Searching:

http://adam.ac.uk/info/boolean.html

Guide to Crafting a Search:

http://www.slu.edu/departments/english/research/

The Big 6 Information Skills Overview

http://www.big6.com/showarticle/php?id=16

Effective Assignments Using Library and Internet Resources

http://www.lib.berkeley.edu/instruct/assignments.html

Instructional Internet Information

http://landmark-%09project.com/page.php?stamp=&pn=8&psn=&cat=30

Comprehensive Tutorial on Searching:

http://www.lib.berkeley.edu/TeachingLib/Guides/Internet/ThingsToKnow.html *and*
http://www.lib.berkeley.edu/TeachingLib/Guides/Internet/FindInfo.html

Search Engine Sites

How to Search the Web by Terry A. Gray

http://daphne.palomar.edu/TGSEARCH/

Six-step Tutorial on Search Engines:

http://www.monash.com/spidap2.html

Evaluating Web Sources

Evaluating Internet Resources:

http://www.virtualsalt.com/evalu8it.htm

Information Literacy Resources by Alan November

http//www.novemberlearning.com/index.php?option=com_content&task=category&sectionid=5&id=27&itemid

Checking Evaluation Criteria for Web Sites:

http://lib.nmsu.edu/instruction/evalcrit.html

Evaluating Information Found on the Internet – Johns Hopkins University

http://www.library.jhu.edu/elp/useit/evaluate/index.html

Thinking Critically About Web Sites:

    http://www.library.ucla.edu/libraries/college/help/critical/index.htm

Citing Web Sources

UC Berkeley Citing Sources:

    http://www.lib.berkeley.edu/TeachingLib/Guides/Internet/Style.html

Citing Web Sources MLA Style by Robert Harris

    http://www.virtualsalt.com/mla.htm

Information Directories

The Learning Page from The Library of Congress

    http://memory.loc.gov/learn/start/site_map.html

Opposing Viewpoints Resource Center

    http://gale.cengage.com/OpposingViewpoints/

Middle School Public Debate Program at Claremont McKenna College

    http://middleschooldebate.com/resources/resourcesmain.htm

Vermont Middle School Debate

    http://debate.uvm.edu.middlewhy.htm

The "Invisible" or "Deep" Web

    http://www.lib.berkeley.edu/TeachingLib/Guides/Internet/InvisibleWeb.html

Supersite collections grouped into six categories:

    http://scout.cs.wisc.edu/addserv/toolkit/searching/index.html

Assessment

Central Michigan Plagiarism Site

    http://www.ehhs.cmich.edu/~mspears/plagiarism.html

Rubrics for Assessment – University of Wisconsin at Stout

    http://www.uwstout.edu/soe/profdev/rubrics.shtml#reports

References

Billig, Michael (1996). *Arguing and thinking.* Cambridge, England: Cambridge University Press.

Bridgeland J., Dilulio, J., Morrison, K. (2006). *The Silent Epidemic: Perspectives of High School Dropouts,* Bill and Melinda Gates Foundation, retrieved from <http://www.gatesfoundation.org/UnitedStates/Education/TransformingHighSchools/RelatedInfo/SilentEpidemicSummit.htm>, February, 2007.

Corsaro, William (2003). *We're friends, right?* Washington, DC: Joseph Henry Press.

Costa, A. and Kallick, B. (2000). *Assessing & Reporting on Habits of Mind.* Alexandria, VA: ASCD.

Crammond, Joanna. (1998). The uses and complexity of argument structures in expert and student persuasive writing. *Written Communication, 15,* 230–268.

Davidson, Josephine. (1997). *The Middle School Debater.* Bellingham, WA: The Right Book Co.

Egelko, B. (May 14, 2007). 'Honk for peace' case tests limits on free speech. *San Francisco Chronicle,* page 1.

Ericson, J., Murphy, J., & Zeuschner, R. (1987). *The Debater's Guide* (3rd ed.) Carbondale, IL: Southern Illinois University Press.

Felton, M. & Kuhn, D. (2001). The development of Argumentative Discourse Skill. *Discourse Processes, 32* (2&3), 135–153.

Felton, M. & Herko, S. (2004). From dialogue to two-sided argument: Scaffolding adolescents' persuasive writing. *Journal of Adolescent & Adult Literacy 47* (8), 672–683.

Fine, Gary. (2001). *Gifted Tongues: High School Debate and Adolescent Culture.* Princeton, NJ: Princeton University Press.

Graff, Gerald. (2003). *Clueless in Academe: How Schooling Obscures the Life of the Mind.* New Haven, CT: Yale University Press.

Gurian, M. & Stevens, K. (2005). *The Minds of Boys.* San Francisco: Jossey-Bass Publishing.

Jensen, Eric. (1998). *Teaching with the brain in mind.* Alexandria, VA: ASCD.

Kuhn, Deanna. (1991) *The Skills of Argument.* New York: Cambridge University Press.

Kuhn, Deanna. (2005). *Education for Thinking.* Cambridge, MA: Harvard University Press.

Meier, Deborah. (2002) *The Power of their ideas.* Boston: Beacon Press.

Monty Python, "The Argument Clinic," transcribed from "The Second [In Sequence, Not in Quality] Monty Python's Flying Circus Videocassette: (Paramount Pictures, 1970, 1972, 1992).

National Center for Educational Statistics. (Nov. 2000). Scoring of Twelfth-Grade Persuasive Writing, *NAEP Facts, 5*(3), retrieved from <http://nces.ed.gov/pubs2000/2000488.pdf> January 30, 2007.

National Center for Educational Statistics. (2002). Writing Highlights 2002, *Nation's Report Card,* retrieved from <http://nces.ed.gov/nationsreportcard/pubs/main2002/2003531.asp> February, 2007.

Sax, Leonard. (2006). *Why Gender Matters.* New York: Broadway Books.

Schmoker, Mike. (2006). *Results Now.* Alexandria, VA: ASCD.

Schmoker, Mike. (2007). Reading, Writing, and Thinking for All. *Educational Leadership, 64(7),* 63–66.

Sousa, David. (2001). *How the Brain Learns* (2nd ed.). Thousand Oaks, CA: Corwin Press, Inc.

Weston, Anthony. (2000). *A Rulebook for Arguments* (3rd ed.). Indianapolis: Hackett Publishing Co.

Wiggins, Grant. (1999). *Assessing Student Performance.* San Francisco: Jossey-Bass Publishing.

Crossword Puzzle Answer Key

Pg 28
Debate Crossword Puzzle

Pg 75
Critical Thinking Crossword Puzzle

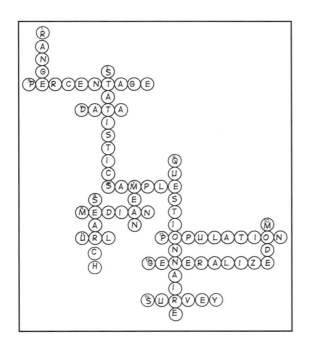

Pg 50
Research Crossword Puzzle

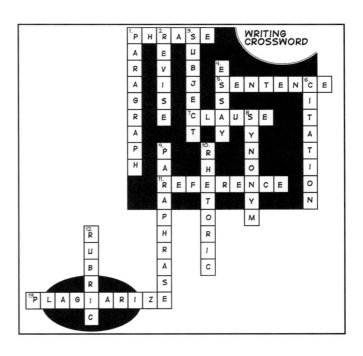

Pg 100
Writing Crossword Puzzle

Dr. Bill McBride

Bill McBride is a well-known national speaker, educator, and author. A former middle and high school reading specialist, English and social studies teacher, Bill presently trains teachers both nationally and internationally in content area reading methodologies and teaching to gender differences. His highly interactive workshops are filled with practical hands-on strategies based on best practices. He holds a Masters in Reading and a Ph.D. in Curriculum and Instruction from the University of North Carolina at Chapel Hill.

Bill has contributed to the development of a number of school textbook series in language arts, social studies and vocabulary development. His latest book on content area reading is *Building Literacy in Social Studies*, written with Donna Ogle and Ron Klemp. He is also known for his heartwarming novel *Entertaining an Elephant*. Already in its sixteenth printing and used by school districts across the nation, the book tells the moving story of a burned-out teacher who becomes re-inspired with both his profession and his life.

You can contact Bill at www.entertaininganelephant.com.